Ecocide

MANCHESTER
1824

Manchester University Press

Ecocide

Kill the corporation before it kills us

David Whyte

Manchester University Press

Published by Manchester University Press
Oxford Road, Manchester M13 9PL
www.manchesteruniversitypress.co.uk

British Library Cataloguing-in-Publication Data
A catalogue record for this book is available from the British Library

ISBN 978 1 5261 4698 4   paperback

First published 2020

Typeset by Servis Filmsetting Ltd, Stockport, Cheshire
Printed in Great Britain by TJ Books Limited, Padstow

Contents

Preface: from COVID-capitalism to survival of the species

There is an almost mythical story of an alternative to capitalist production, developed by workers in the British arms industry in the 1970s and 1980s, that is sometimes hazily recalled by older political activists. It is a story that should be dusted down and its lessons re-learned as a guide to our times. The 'combine plan' developed by a large number of unionised engineering workers – employed by the arms corporation Lucas Aerospace – is one that seems more and more incredible as the years go by.[1] Those workers, fed up with their skills being used to produce weapons, developed prototypes of a number of socially useful technologies. Many of their inventions were groundbreaking and were not fully developed for many years: wind turbines, electric vehicles and a type of energy-efficient heat pump that is now widely used. The list goes on and on. Those workers were responding innovatively to the collapse of the British manufacturing industry and sought to harness the country's capacity for making the things that were really needed, not merely the things that could really sell. Tragically, despite the detailed plans and business cases, and the revolutionary inventions that came together years ahead of their time, the 'Lucas Plan' failed to gain the support of government or private investors.

Some of the industries that today bear the most blame for the climate crisis, including auto manufacture, air transport and the arms industry, are all likely to suffer major long-term losses as a result of the COVID-19 crisis. They could do with a 'Lucas Plan'. On the manufacturing side, the UK company Rolls Royce is projected to lose 8,000 jobs; and all of the major airlines are projecting thousands upon thousands of job losses. The human tragedy of the virus will be immeasurably compounded by the economic fallout. Yet, our commitment to a booming, carbon-based air transport sector seems absurd at the moment, as does the scale of public investment in arms.[2] And yet, there are signs that repurposing both transport and arms companies in this day and age might not only be possible but essential.[3] At the onset of the COVID-19 pandemic in the UK, British military giant BAE Systems very quickly started producing essential medical supplies, including face masks and ventilation units.[4] Although the examples of an immediate switch in production are relatively small, such cases do show the potential we have to transform our economy.

However, none of the economic measures introduced by advanced capitalist states in response to COVID-19 have seriously sought to make our economy more sustainable. Indeed, governments around the world, rather than taking a Lucas-style approach, have only one solution: protect the system as it is!

Initial 'business support packages' in Europe were valued at around 15% of GDP in countries like Spain, Germany, France and the UK. The final value, which we will all pay for in the long run, will certainly be much more. In the US, just three months into the crisis, the bailout was valued at around three times the total for government-backed funds made available following the 2008 economic crash. They are called 'business support packages' because that is exactly what they are: wage subsidies (most of those payments went to corporate payroll departments rather than directly to workers); large government-backed loans; and one-off payments to keep transport and infrastructure corporations afloat. Another tranche went to the self-employed and small businesses, largely to maintain a labour market based on the casualised and cheap labour that our major corporations thrive on.

An iron rule of corporate capitalism has been revealed by this crisis again, perhaps more clearly than before: the profit-making corporations at the heart of the system can only survive economic shocks if they are kept on life support, by us. The scale of this life-support effort has revealed to us how possible, and indeed necessary, a major economic transformation might be. Yet, at this undeniably decisive point for the future of the planet, no one is asking how we use the immense resources being thrown at COVID-19 to precipitate a social transformation that does not involve reproducing the means of our own self-destruction. This is precisely the question asked and answered in full by the Lucas Aerospace workers. With 40 years of hindsight, now, more than ever before, we need to ask the most fundamental questions about how we can survive as a species.

There is, at the same time, a sinister, 'hidden' aspect of this bailout. In many countries around the world, there has been a silent crusade against the safety and environmental standards that corporations are expected to meet. European car manufacturers have been demanding subsidies to ensure survival, and, in the very same breath, have been lobbying hard for CO_2 emission standards to be lowered.[5] In Canada, oil and gas companies have been pushing to lift environmental regulations, and the Keystone XL pipeline to facilitate the extraction of high carbon oil from tar sands was approved with a \$5 billion subsidy.[6] In the US, the government has used the crisis to speed up the repeal of environmental laws and the sale of land to oil and gas mining and timber corporations.[7] The US Environmental Protection Agency has suspended enforcement of environmental laws. The Chinese government gifted its coal industry with an unprecedented mass issue of new mining permits. Many US states lifted rules on single-use plastics. In England, the ban on plastic straws was postponed and plastic manufacturers in Europe are fighting hard to shelve the ban on plastic forks. The list goes on and on.

Most galling for some has been that many of the

stimulus packages prioritised some of the worst environmental offenders. The Bank of England's qualitative easing programme included BP and Rio Tinto, of whom we will hear more later in the book. Why, when those sectors are clearly failing and are unable to withstand the shock, is our government's automatic reflex to protect investors at our expense? Why is the government's auto-reflex not to protect our environmental standards, but to support the fossil fuel industry and weaken existing regulation and controls that could help us reverse climate change and the ecological crisis?

Crispin Odey, who made an estimated £115 million from the crisis by betting on market failure in March 2020, has also invested heavily in projects that destroy the environment. In February, Odey increased his stake in Brazilian firm SLC Agricola, a corporation that has been revealed to have a stake in deforestation. The system of investment that determines what is valued, and who makes money from crises, is cyclical. Social disasters reap profits which are then ploughed into environmental disasters, producing more social disasters, and on and on it goes – a sick game that we can only stand back and watch.

It is difficult to see how this predatory cycle of investment can be broken. Odey is unusual in the sense that most investors are able to remain completely anonymous. Indeed, if you want to remain removed and distant from the source of your wealth, you can. This is the real scandal of social distancing that we need to talk about in light of COVID-19, since, as this book will show, this feature of capitalist systems has a more pernicious and central role in destroying our planet than we ever acknowledge.

The COVID-19 crisis has put into sharper focus the stark choice we face for the future of the planet. We can choose to depart from the crisis by developing a sustainable economy and sustainable jobs: a green industrial revolution. Or, we can simply allow the biggest corporations to win again and strip away any environmental regulations that stand meekly in their way. There are obvious alternatives to the way our failed systems are organised. We have a whole range of other models, tried and successfully tested in different countries, normally after things have failed in the past. From Argentina to the Basque Country and Catalonia, we could recite an ABC of alternatives to capitalist production that have been created by people just to survive the economic shocks of the twenty-first century. We know from real, lived, human experience in the aftermath of economic crises, that protecting corporations and their investors is not the only way to organise an economy.

The problem is that they would mean removing the right of the ultimate beneficiaries of the corporation – investors – to profit in perpetuity. It would also mean removing the rights and privileges of their most senior managers and directors. In other words, dealing with the corporation means precipitating a fundamental shift in the balance of social classes. It means overturning the social position of elites.

COVID-19 is one of many global tragedies we will witness in our lifetime. Yet it is because of its global nature that we have no choice but to recognise the nuts and bolts of how pandemics like this germinate. There is clear evidence that new strains of viruses like COVID-19 are only able to move between species in large-scale 'factory' meat farms.[8] It is no coincidence that our most recent outbreaks were 'swine-flu' (H1-N1) and 'bird-flu' (H5-N1). Those are the most intensely farmed animals and that are kept in environments that are of a scale that allow viruses to mutate from animals to humans. What are those industries characterised by? The domination of large corporations. Huge global pork producers like Smithfield and poultry producers like Tyson and Doux have led a revolution in meat production that is based upon growing the scale and intensity of farms.[9] This is not to say that those corporations are responsible for COVID-19 or any other virus. Rather, it is a particular model of capitalism that is at fault, and this model creates the conditions that simultaneously allow corporations to dominate and viruses to spread. At one level this is an unfortunate coincidence. But given that the domination of the sector by large corporations facilitates and encourages viral conditions, the reality of the situation is that we need to break this model of corporate capitalism if we are to have any chance of controlling future outbreaks.

If we cannot contemplate such a basic human need as food production outside the structure of corporate capitalism after what we have just been through, then we are destined to face the ultimate human existential threat. Indeed, as this book will argue, if we don't imagine food production, energy, transport and indeed all extractive and manufacturing industries outside the structure of corporate capitalism, then we reduce our chances of humans surviving as a species catastrophically.

Long after the COVID-19 crisis has passed, future generations will look at this period as a 'moment' that everything might have changed direction; a moment that woke us up to the fact that we could not live side-by-side with corporations. They will question why we did not break the back of a corporate structure that is killing us. Most of all, they will question why we did not kill the corporation when we had the chance.

David Whyte
May 2020

Acknowledgements

I am grateful to the great many people who helped me with ideas and sources over the course of writing this book. The introduction benefitted from detailed revisions suggested by Vickie Cooper who has supported me with both the warmest loving support and the coldest intellectual criticism throughout the writing of the book. Thank you x.

Lara Montesinos Coleman made a number of incisive modifications on an early version of the manuscript. Chapter 2 was read by Rob Knox, and chapter 3 by Steve Tombs, both of whom provided invaluable suggestions. Tom Dark, commissioning editor at Manchester University Press, diligently pored over the manuscript and used his impressively sharp editorial skills to revise and reshape the text. He was also instrumental in molding the project from the beginning of the process to the end.

People I have written with in recent years who helped me to hone the ideas contained in this book include: Jose Atiles, Ignasi Bernat, Stéfanie Khoury, Anne Alvesalo-Kuusi and my long-standing collaborator

Steve Tombs, who may recognise some phrases herein that may or may not have been ripped-off from him. I am grateful to Polly Higgins, who did so much work in rehabilitating the concept of ecocide before her tragic death in 2019. I also acknowledge a great debt to everyone who has been involved in the discussions, debates and conversations that shaped the arguments developed in this book. They include: Grietja Baars, Joel Benjamin, Monish Bhatia, Steve Bittle, Jon Burnett, Pablo Ciocchini, Ben Crawford, Keith Ewing, Kevin Farnsworth, Alejandro Forero, Harry Glasbeek, Fiona Haines, Paddy Ireland, Dani Jiménez, Ciara Kierans, Cad Jones, Liisa Lähteenmäki, Hanna Malik, Russell Mokhiber, Andrew Moretta, Hilda Palmer, Frank Pearce, Gustavo Rojas-Páez, Vicki Sentas, Laureen Snider, Susanne Soederberg, Viviana Tacha, Richard Whittell, Jess Whyte, Jörg Wiegratz and the Socialist Register collective.

Thanks to all of the universities and other organisations that gave me the space to test out my ideas along the way. They include: the School of Social and Political Sciences, University of York; the Department of Criminology, Birkbeck; the Universidad de Castilla-La Mancha; the University of Barcelona; the International Institute for the Sociology of Law, Oñati; the University of Turku; the School of African and Oriental Studies Law School; the University of Bristol Law School; RMIT Melbourne; the Research Committee for the Sociology of Law; the European Group for the Study of Deviance and Social Control; Corporate Watch;

and the CUP Escola D'estiu, Catalonia. The work in this book was supported by a Leverhulme Trust Major Research Fellowship (MRF-2016-091).

The great socio-legal scholar, W.G. (Kit) Carson, died as this book went to press. I discussed some of the ideas in chapters 2 and 3 with him in March 2019, the last time I saw him. Kit Carson had a profound influence on the approach adopted here, much more than I could ever acknowledge. The book is dedicated to him. Thanks, Kit.

Introduction: corporate ecocide

The world's first known corporation was a Swedish mining company called Stora Kopparberg. The founding certificate of the company, dated 1288, is the earliest documented evidence of a profit-making corporation. It was established by German merchants as a means of investing in a copper mine in the town of Falun and it was a roaring success. In the seventeenth century, two thirds of European copper production took place in Falun, and the mine remained an important site for copper production until it closed in the 1990s. The site of the Falun mine is now on the UNESCO World Heritage list. The idea that the world's first corporation was born in Sweden has been a matter of national pride over the years. Stora Kopparberg's founding documents were part of the Swedish exhibition at the 1964 World Fair in New York and are now held in the National Archive in Stockholm. Remarkably, the corporation still exists today. In its present-day guise, Stora Kopparberg (now known as Stora Enso) is the second largest paper producer in the world and is based in Helsinki.

The mine has left an enduring mark on its environment. Scientific studies of the surrounding areas reveal that both land and watercourses have been permanently damaged. One study by Swedish researchers concluded that the lakes are acidified and unlikely to recover,[1] and that extremely high metal concentrations in the soil[2] indicate very long-lasting and perhaps irreversible environmental damage.[3] As we shall see in subsequent chapters, in recent years, Stora Enso has also been accused of causing significant damage to biodiversity in forests across the world. And so the legacy continues. Yet at no point in its long history has Stora Kopparberg had to face questions about its environmental record, let alone pay the costs of a clean-up or compensation for any damage it has caused. Indeed, in its modern incarnation, Stora Enso seems to have managed to escape any association with the Falun mine or its legacy. As this book will show, this is the point of the corporation. It enables investors to walk away from the damage caused by their activities without ever having to face the consequences.

The Stora story will unfold in more detail throughout this book. As we shall discover, the story of the world's first profit-making corporation symbolises the fundamental problem that this book seeks to confront: no matter how much destruction corporations cause to us and our environment, they are designed to survive and thrive in perpetuity.

This book is about ecocide, the deliberate destruction of our natural environment. Ecocide as a term captures the entirety of the threats to the sustainability of the planet: climate change, the ravaging of ecosystems, the eradication of species and the pollution of air, land and water. The book will argue that it is impossible to avert ecocide as long as corporations remain in control of the industrial processes that are wrecking our world.

Capitalism, ecocide and the corporation

As the book progresses, we will discover exactly why the contemporary form of the profit-making corporation is probably as close as we could get to a model organisation that is capable of destroying the world. If this sounds like a description of SPECTRE, the evil organisation from the Bond films, or Marvel's A.I.M., then in many ways the truth is more terrifying than fiction. The book will show how the profit-making corporation, the form of organisation that dominates contemporary capitalism, evolved into the deadliest human invention – an invention that has accelerated the capacity for the destruction of the planet in ways its creators could never have imagined.

There is a critique of capitalism at the core of the movement against climate change led by groups like Climate Camp, Extinction Rebellion and in the school students' movement, FridaysforFuture. On the Global Climate Strike on 20 September 2019, some of the most used slogans directed attention at capitalism: "System change not climate change!"; "Capitalism kills our future!"; and "el capitalismo mata el planeta!" This growing movement is putting the way that the *capitalist* system organises our economy, and the way that it makes and consumes things, to the forefront of the struggle against climate change. A nascent movement against climate change within the trade union movement is also driven by a critique of capitalism.[4]

This movement is absolutely right in its critique. Understanding how capitalism works is a crucial starting point for understanding the driving forces behind the eco-crisis. Capitalism as a system is based on perpetual growth and the continual reproduction of private wealth. And for reasons explored in this book, in the capitalist system, the protection of the environment is always subordinated to the accumulation of profit for a privileged elite.

The relationship between capitalism and ecocide becomes clear when we analyse the logics and the practices of *capital.* Indeed, the book will show that the corporation – the mechanism that capital uses to reproduce itself – was designed in a way that virtually guarantees ecocide. Understanding the capitalist corporation and then doing something about it must therefore be at the centre of the struggle to control climate change and the ecological crisis.

Ecocide is a term that is increasingly being used in the renewed protest movement against climate change. Indeed, the proposal to make ecocide a crime has become one of the demands of Extinction Rebellion;[5] it has become a topic of interest for academic lawyers and criminologists,[6] and has influenced criminal law in a small number of states.[7]

The profit-making corporation was at the heart of the political debates that gave birth to the concept of "ecocide" almost half a century ago. In 1972 Olof Palme, the Prime Minister of Sweden, used the concept to describe the use of napalm and the defoliant Agent Orange during the Vietnam War. Chemical warfare in Vietnam was being used to slaughter people in enemy territory, destroy their villages and wipe out forests and crops.[8] Palme, along with other world leaders including Indian Prime Minister Indira Gandhi called for ecocide to be an international crime and, subsequently, international lawyer Richard Falk published a draft Ecocide Convention directly in response to those calls.[9] Though it was never adopted, the Convention provided the legal basis for outlawing the use of chemical substances to clear people from the land in wartime or peacetime.

It is estimated that 4.8 million people were directly sprayed with Agent Orange[10] and around 400,000 people died immediately. The Vietnamese Red Cross estimates that a further 1 million people were disabled or suffered severe health problems,[11] and Vietnamese babies are still being born today with congenital disorders caused by the persistence of the chemical in the biosphere. The chemical was sprayed on almost a fifth of the land mass of Vietnam, and tree stocks and animal life are still severely depleted in those areas and unlikely to recover.[12]

Nine different private chemical companies, led by Monsanto, had been given the job of developing and manufacturing Agent Orange for the US military.[13] There have been a number of legal actions taken against those companies, specifically, Dow, Monsanto and Diamond Shamrock. Those companies have, like the US military, continued to deny any relationship between health effects on claimants and their chemicals. Most of the class actions have been settled out of court. The US government continues to deny the effects of Agent Orange on the Vietnamese people and the persistent poisoning of land and water supplies.[14] The fact that corporations played a central role in the Vietnamese ecocide is not peripheral or coincidental; it cannot be reduced to a footnote in history. As we shall discover in the book, corporations are playing the central role in the global ecocide that we face now.

It is important to be clear about what is meant by the term "corporation". It is used in this book to mean any profit-making organisation that is "incorporated" as an entity that is separate from its shareholders or investors. This means any for-profit organisation that has the status of a separate "person" in law (something we will explore in some detail in chapter 1 of this book) from the people that have a financial stake in it either as owners of shareholders.[15]

Most of the world's key commodities are owned and controlled by corporations.[16] It is estimated that since 1965, 20 corporations have collectively produced 35% of all fossil fuel emissions;[17] since 1988, just

100 have collectively produced 71% of all fossil fuel emissions.[18] The biggest offenders are: ExxonMobil, Shell, BP and Chevron. Almost all of the plastic that is choking our oceans is produced by for-profit corporations. Greenpeace has listed the biggest offenders as Coca-Cola, PepsiCo, Nestlé, Danone, Mondelez International, Procter & Gamble, Unilever, Perfetti van Melle, Mars and Colgate-Palmolive. It is estimated that 60% of Coca-Cola's packaging is single use plastic.[19] Most ambient air pollution – the air pollution caused by particles released into the environment when fuel is used or other things are burned – is produced by profit-making corporations.[20] Ambient air pollution is a major killer, contributing to 4.2 million early deaths every year.[21] The deadliest chemicals in our water and air – such as pesticides and dioxins – are also produced almost entirely by profit-making corporations.[22]

Perhaps the most systematic study of the influence of corporations in the global economy has been conducted by researchers at the Swiss Federal Institute of Technology in Zurich. The researchers analysed the ownership patterns of over 37 million corporations and investors worldwide to map exactly who owns what. This mapping exercise revealed that 737 corporations control about 80% of the wealth; and 147 corporations controlled about 40%. In other words, most of the world's wealth is controlled by a relatively small network of elite corporations.[23] And since this seminal study was conducted, the market concentration of corporate structures has increased significantly.[24]

This small network of elite corporations are the key agents in climate change and the eco-crisis. It is this small network that is killing us.

Conspicuous by its absence

Yet the central role played by the *corporate* economy in this eco-crisis has been conspicuously absent from the public debate. The role that the corporation plays in this looming catastrophe is almost always ignored in the most significant scientific reports on climate change and global pollution. Pick up any of the reports by the UN or the international financial institutions, or indeed any of the global health organisations, and you will not see any discussion of the corporation's role in the growing environmental catastrophe.

The Paris Agreement,[25] for example, includes no acknowledgement of the key role that profit-making corporations play in climate change. It fails to mention the words "corporation", "company", "profit", or indeed make any reference to the key roles played by corporate management or corporate investors in the text. Precisely the same can be said about all of the key manuals, reports and agreements on this subject that are produced by international organisations. The detailed manual supporting the Kyoto Protocol included no reference to those terms, with one exception. A solitary footnote asserts that "an entity can be a company, plant or broker authorized by a Party to hold or trade in emissions". The Kyoto Protocol therefore only mentions corporations when it asserts their role as participants in the new system of emissions trading that was established by the Treaty.[26]

Other key climate change reports mention corporations only in passing. When they are mentioned, it is only in the context of their positive contribution to policy or carbon-reduction strategies, such as in the Intergovernmental Panel on Climate Change's seminal *Special Report on Global Warming of 1.5°*.[27] We can say the same thing about other key 'official' documents on the eco-crisis, including the World Bank's *Climate Change Action Plan*,[28] the World Health Organization's *Reducing Global Health Risks Through the Mitigation of Short-lived Climate Pollutants*[29] and the International Agency for Research on Cancer's *Air Pollution and Cancer*.[30]

Any efforts to reduce climate change are bound to fail unless we confront the reality that the vast majority of the major threats to our environment are currently produced and controlled by profit-making corporations. Yet in the international treaties, and in many of the radical proposals to transform our economy, corporations are either envisaged as a solution to the crisis, or are ignored completely.

We can make a similar observation about the agenda that has emerged to promote a "green new deal" and a "green industrial revolution". Take, for example, the proposal presented by the US politician Alexandria Ocasio-Cortez, setting out how the

US government could create a green new deal.[31] The proposal is extensive and radical, and it sets out a blueprint for the transformation of the economy. Yet it stops short of making any proposals for the reform of the corporate economy. Of course, the context is important here. This proposal was tabled in the second legislature of the world's leading capitalist nation, the US House of Representatives. Because of this, Ocasio-Cortez is understandably being strategic about her targets.

In other versions of the green new deal, developed in places that do not need to be so politically cautious or strategic, we still find a lack of discussion about the corporation as a problem that needs to be confronted head-on. In the international trade union movement, the adoption of green new deal proposals tend to be based on the idea that a just transition to a carbon neutral economy can be achieved *in partnership* with corporations. Environmental historian Stefania Barca has shown that the International Trade Union Confederation and the International Labour Organisation promote a sustainable version of capitalism that can be achieved through "dialogue and democratic consultation" with "social partners and stakeholders".[32] Through this process, corporations are persuaded to come to their senses and change their ways. In short, the dominant approach that is currently present in trade union demands for a green new deal would mean the continuation of a model of capitalism which retains the profit-making corporation as its main protagonist. This approach will not be enough to protect workers in supply chains with global corporations at the head. There is powerful evidence that the intensification of labour in agricultural supply chains, combined with rising global temperatures, has already given rise to deadly new occupational diseases.[33]

This book will argue that a viable green new deal will have to contend with the problem of corporate power head-on. New forms of organisation must replace rather than sit alongside profit-making, share-owned corporations, because, as this book will show, the latter are incapable of contributing to a sustainable economy.

After attending the UN General Assembly in September 2019, the anti-Apartheid leader, Archbishop Desmond Tutu, clearly disappointed by the lack of any discussion of the role of the corporate economy, demanded that corporations and financial institutions "must pull us back from the climate abyss". The corporate sector must, he argued, "reinvent itself by gravitating to sustainable investment in both developed and developing markets". If they don't, he argued "activists must insist that they do it".[34]

Beetles and monkeys

There must be executives and corporations who are prepared to reinvent the corporate sector presently, but as this book will argue, they are not likely to change the tide. We now have a century's worth of very detailed evidence that tells us exactly how corporate executives – and investors – respond to the discovery of very serious problems with their products. Unfortunately, this evidence does not allow us to draw very optimistic conclusions about the likelihood of the corporate sector reinventing itself.

The story of how tobacco executives distorted and denied evidence of the link between smoking and cancer is well known. Medical research linking smoking to lung cancer began to appear in the 1920s. In the early 1950s, as it became apparent that the mounting evidence could threaten its interests, the tobacco companies organised a major campaign to disrupt scientific research, and to lie about and distort medical evidence.[35] Similarly, the mineral asbestos was known as "killer dust" in the nineteenth century and all of the main manufacturers systematically hid evidence of the death toll for more than a century.[36]

We can observe precisely the same pattern in countless other industries.[37] The Volkswagen "dieselgate" case which broke in 2015 is perhaps the best-known environmental scandal to hit the corporate sector in recent years. The case involved the use of software to fraudulently understate deadly NOx emissions from 11 million cars. The real level of NOx emissions in Volkswagen, Audi and Porsche cars was up to 40 times more than the test results showed, and research subsequently showed that this pollution led to around 1,200 premature deaths.[38] It seems incredible now, but prior to dieselgate, Volkswagen was regarded as an arche-typal environmentally friendly company.[39]

In terms of the sheer scale of the fraud, and the scale of the air pollution it produced, it is a case that revealed a lot about the way that corporate capital-ism works. Two events that occurred either side of the scandal breaking are especially revealing. In 2014, the year before the dieselgate story broke, Volkswagen had commissioned a series of tests that involved plac-ing 10 Java monkeys in small airtight chambers for four hours watching cartoons as they breathed in diesel fumes from a VW Beetle. Internal company documents revealed that similar tests had been conducted on human subjects.[40] The Beetle was one of the cars fitted with a defeat device, and therefore would have pro-duced misleading results. We do not know precisely the purpose of the research but we do know that the results would almost certainly have distorted the envi-ronmental and human toll of emissions.

One of the first things that Volkswagen did after the first news stories began to emerge in summer 2015 was commission its own engineers to test other brands.[41] The company's executives knew that one way of deflecting attention and mitigating the blame was to dish the dirt on the whole industry. Volkswagen put their research team on the job because they assumed something that the rest of us didn't: the falsification of diesel emissions had been common practice across the industry for years. The aim was to prove that cheating was normal across the industry and therefore mitigate

Volkswagen's guilt and reduce its exposure to litigation. Of course, its assumption was correct. As well as having been fitted to Volkswagen brands, we know now that "defeat" devices were used by Fiat Chrysler,[42] Nissan,[43] Renault,[44] Mercedes[45] and Mitsubishi[46] amongst others.

The car industry would require a much bigger book than this one just to summarise the extent to which all of the major manufacturers have covered up and distorted evidence of environmental and human harm over the years.[47] The classic case study of corporate crime that is still used widely in business school classrooms is the example of the Ford Pinto.[48] But in reality, examples like the Ford Pinto – in which known, potentially deadly, safety flaws were denied and covered up – happen so routinely in the industry they are barely noticed now.[49] It is likely Volkswagen's response to dieselgate will feature as a model case study in business school corporate social responsibility and marketing courses for years to come. Why? Because Volkswagen not only survived this crisis, but came out of it with restored revenues and a barely dented reputation.[50]

Burying the bodies

The major oil companies have been manipulating the evidence of climate change for decades, at least since the 1970s. Exxon executives were presented with evidence by its own scientists in 1977 which estimated that "a doubling of the carbon dioxide concentration in the atmosphere would increase average global temperatures by 2 to 3 degrees Celsius".[51] The company then embarked on an intensive programme of research that sampled CO_2 emissions and conducted rigorous climate modelling. In 1981, the research programme concluded: "An expanded R&D program does not appear to offer significantly increased benefits"[52] and the research was quietly ditched. From the early 1990s onwards corporate funding by Exxon and by the Koch Family Foundations directly financed groups that attacked climate change science and policy solutions.[53] This research sowed enough polarisation and doubt around climate change science to ensure that political recognition of the problem of climate change was significantly downplayed.[54] Subsequently, environmental campaigners have discovered that the propaganda battle around climate change involved extensive covert surveillance and spying on them by Big Oil.[55]

One of the first warning signs about climate change came to the world's attention when scientists began to understand the effects of chlorofluorocarbons (CFCs), the chemicals used in a range of products including aerosols and fridges, air conditioning and all-purpose packaging and furniture products like Styrofoam. In 1974, two significant scientific studies demonstrated that a build-up of CFCs was responsible for depleting the ozone layer, essential for absorbing the sun's ultraviolet radiation and cooling down the earth. Indeed, the studies concluded that the effects were most probably irreversible. It is unlikely that chemical companies manufacturing CFCs knew, or could have known, the irreversible effects of their product before 1974. Yet, as soon as the findings were published, the US Chemical Manufacturers Association, led by the chemical company, DuPont (the main commercial developer of CFCs), initiated a research programme by academic investigators to obtain their own results. The industry urged caution, and, promising it would step up the search for a safe alternative chemical, did everything it could to delay a regulatory ban on CFCs.[56] In 1980, as soon as it became obvious that a global ban was on its way, DuPont withdrew all research funding for its safe alternative.[57] It was not until 1986, after British scientists had discovered a gaping hole in the ozone layer over Antarctica, that DuPont re-committed to finding an alternative, and later the company was to support a phase out of CFCs by 2000. James Lovelock, the British scientist who had discovered the problem of CFC build-up in 1971, noted with regret almost 50 years later: "Manufacturers were determined to deny they had any effects on the global environment, notably the depletion of the ozone layer in the atmosphere".[58]

The manipulation of the science of climate change and ozone depletion reveals a pattern of corporate denial and deliberate cover-up that seems to prevail, even when the evidence becomes irrefutable. This is a pattern that has also typified the production of our most persistent and damaging chemicals. Here are just a few examples.

• *Leaded petrol.* The deadly effects of adding lead compounds to petrol was discovered by scientists in the

1920s. Despite this knowledge, a trio of major corporations: General Motors, DuPont (both of CFC fame) and Standard Oil of New Jersey (now ExxonMobil) ensured that almost all research on the health effects of lead in petrol was funded by the oil companies, and produced findings which concluded that lead additives were not harmful.[59] They then aggressively marketed and promoted the addition of tetraethyl-lead until it was banned in the 1990s.[60]

- *Bisphenol A (BPA).* BPA is a plastic that has been known to mimic oestrogen and cause hormonal damage to humans since the 1930s.[61] The American Chemistry Council consistently sought to cast doubt over scientific studies.[62] The result was that BPA production continued to grow and is still widely used in food and drink packaging.[63]

- *Polychlorinated biphenyl (PCB).* Monsanto was the principle manufacturer of PCB, a chemical used as a coolant and lubricator in electrical equipment when irrefutable evidence of its health impacts came to the attention of the company in 1969. Research showed that those chemicals cause cancer and a wide range of serious health effects, and that they were killing birds and other species.[64] Monsanto's response was to commission a number of research papers based on falsified and distorted results which denied the health and environmental impact of PCB and other chemicals it was manufacturing.[65] Those studies were successful in delaying the banning of PCB for a decade.

- *Polyvinyl chloride (PVC)*. In 1973, an internal Ethyl Corporation memo noted lab results showing a "positive carcinogenic effect" produced by exposure to vinyl chloride, the chemical used to produce the polymer, polyvinyl chloride (PVC).[66] And yet, well into the 1990s, US chemical companies continued to conspire and manipulate the results of scientific studies on PVC production to avoid liability for worker exposure, refusing to warn local communities that chemical spills of vinyl chloride could be deadly.[67]

- *Organophosphates*. The devastating effects of organophosphate pesticides have always been known. It is estimated that 3 million people are poisoned and 300,000 are killed every year by this substance.[68] Yet the industry has doubled its efforts under the Trump administration to prevent new regulation to limit the use of organophosphates by urging selective use of data in Federal government reviews. Key manufacture Dow AgroSciences, in particular, has funded a major lobbying effort to block government reviews of the evidence.[69] Sales by major manufacturers, including DuPont, Syngenta, Bayer CropScience AG, BASF SE, Cheminova AS, Yara International, and of course, Dow AgroSciences, continue to rise.[70]

- *Glyphosate*. A recent court action on behalf of 11,000 victims of Monsanto's Roundup weed killer revealed that the corporation spent 10s of millions of dollars on deceptive PR campaigns, ghost-written scientific studies and placed news stories. Documents from the trial showed that in the 1980s EPA studies showed that mice dosed with glyphosate developed rare kidney tumours. After strong lobbying by Monsanto, the US Environmental Protection Agency ignored its own evidence and declared to the public that glyphosate poses no cancer risk. Glyphosate has become the most widely used weed killer precisely because of industry claims it is safer to use than other products.[71]

The chemicals discussed here are known as persistent organic pollutants, or "bio-accumulative" because they are resistant to environmental degradation and therefore accumulate in the biosphere over time.[72] They accumulate in our eco-systems and continue to kill living organisms, for a very, very long time. The knowledge that could have protected us from those toxins has been distorted, devalued and very deliberately buried. And countless bodies have been buried along with this knowledge.

Subsequently, the outcome for the corporations has pretty much been the same as it was for Volkswagen: unharmed, or even improved, market share and revenues. In most cases, the corporations in control of those threats continued to do their utmost to hide everything they knew from us, to deceive us and to produce alternative, "official", scientific results that proved in numbers, equation or lab tests, that there was nothing to see here.

Conclusion: taking the corporation seriously

The big question we are asking here is: if all of those deadly industrial processes are financed, manufactured and distributed under the control of profit-making corporations, then why are corporations not seen as central to the planet's problems?

I don't mean this in the sense of apportioning "blame" or responsibility (although I will discuss the connected issues of liability and impunity in more detail in chapters 1 and 3), but just in a practical sense. Dealing with the fallout of industrial production and consumption means taking the role that the major producers and consumers play in all of this seriously. The central role played by the corporation is of crucial importance to the dynamics of the climate crisis and the ecocide that the planet faces. Yet we persist in allowing all of the substances and industrial processes that are threatening the end of the species to be financed, manufactured and distributed by profit-making corporations.

Let us just reflect on this point, since it presents us with a very significant blind spot in the debate about climate change and the eco-crisis. The corporation is a major threat to us, yet it is a threat that we are not taking seriously enough. If the threats to our environment are left under the control of CEOs and capitalist investors, acting through corporations, all we will be able to do is appeal to their better judgement. The tactic of asking politely is doomed to fail. The evidence that I have so far described indicates that we have a problem that cannot simplistically be dismissed as the fault of a few "rogue" or "bad apple" corporations. In all of the examples mentioned here – fossil fuels, tobacco, asbestos, synthetic chemicals and the car industry – one thing stands out. Very large numbers of corporate executives who were in charge of making deadly products knew exactly what they were doing. Executives wilfully ignored and actively sought to bury the evidence of their killer trade. They were fully aware of the consequences of what they were doing, but did it anyway.

Indeed, as this book will show, those executives were doing the job that the corporate system expects of them. The entity of the corporation has been specifically designed and adopted to ensure the fast and uninhibited reproduction of profit, with little regard for the environmental and social costs. The purpose of this book, then, is to take the corporation seriously. This book will show, categorically, that we will not survive if we continue to allow corporations to occupy a central role in the economy.

What is the corporation?

The immortal person

As we saw in the last chapter, Stora Kopparberg, the world's first known corporation, still exists almost 800 years after it was established. In exchange for the rights to a mine that was on land owned by the church, the German merchants who established Stora Kopparberg gave the Bishop of Västerås a share of the proceeds. Share certificates were issued which gave their bearer the right to operate and profit from the mine. It is for this reason that historians believe Stora Kopparberg is the earliest example of a "joint-stock" corporation, a rudimentary form of the corporate model that dominates capitalism today. The structure of the firm has adapted over the years as its shares have been inherited and sold on through the generations, as new assets have been acquired, and new businesses developed. It is through this process of adaptation that its assets and shareholdings came to be subsumed as part of the present-day Helsinki-based timber and paper giant Stora Enso.

The firm's longevity is remarkable, yet most probably it would not surprise historians who study the corporation. Longevity is one of the most important historical realities of the corporation; the corporation is granted a life in perpetuity. In other words, in the sense that it has no mortal life, the corporation is able to live forever. Once it is "incorporated", the corporation will not die unless it is killed. And it can only be killed by some form of state intervention or legal procedure that liquidates it.

"Incorporation" is effectively the birth of the corporation; it entails a process of recognition or registration by a state government or regulatory authority. When the corporation is registered, this gives it a legal status as an independent "entity", separate from its members or shareholders. This independent status is generally known as "corporate personhood". The "corporate person" (a shorthand expression that describes the way that the corporation is embodied in law[1]) is therefore granted a 'life' that is separate from the lives of its members or shareholders.

An early advantage to investors that resulted from corporate personhood was the ability to evade death duties. People living in Britain have had to pay death duties on their property since they were introduced at the end of the seventeenth century. However, the corporation allowed for a legal sleight of hand. In law, it is the corporate person, not shareholders or "members", that owns the property and assets of the corporation. A deceased owner or investor would not therefore be liable to pay taxes on assets owned by the corporate person.[2] Similarly, if a partner or shareholder became bankrupt, the entity's assets could not be used to pay the debts as the assets belonged to the entity rather than the mere mortal individual shareholder. In this way, by creating an entity – a corporation – that has legal autonomy, individual investors can be exempted from the liabilities or losses associated with the corporation. Unless the corporation goes bankrupt, corporate personhood therefore allows the investments of real persons to keep on working for them even after things have gone badly wrong.

The immortality embodied by the corporate person has a major drawback. Even when the worst atrocities committed against human beings authored by corporations have been exposed, the corporation tends to survive, often remaining alive and kicking long after the people it has killed and maimed are dead. The majority of the corporations mentioned in the introduction to this book, corporations whose executives may have been knowingly responsible for countless deaths and injuries, are still thriving. Few executives and none of the investors paid for their part in those atrocities; and the corporations themselves continue to sell deadly products.

Corporate longevity and human atrocity

The durability of the corporation, no matter the extremity of its actions, is perhaps most graphically illustrated by what happened to the German economy

and to German corporations following World War
II. Perhaps the most famous example is the corporation that was a reference point in the last chapter,
Volkswagen. The car company, now the second largest
in the world as measured by car sales, was created by
Hitler's Third Reich. During the war, Volkswagen used
slave labour from the concentration camps. Indeed, by
the time it was seized by the British Army in 1945,
80% of Volkswagen's workers were slaves. The corporation was returned to the German government in
1948.[3]

The huge industrial conglomerate, I.G. Farben, also
drew its workforce from the concentration camps
throughout the 1940s. In 1943, almost half of I.G.
Farben's workforce of 330,000 was made up of slave
labourers from the concentration camps or of con-
scripts, including around 30,000 from Auschwitz.[4] It
was an I.G. Farben subsidiary that supplied Zyklon B,
the gas that killed over a million people in the holocaust. After World War II, in a case that departed from
the norm, the military tribunals at the Nuremburg trials
prosecuted 23 of the firm's directors for war crimes
(of those, 13 were convicted). Rather than wholly dis-
solving the corporation, it was split up into 6 separate
parts. Other companies profiting from slave labour had
assets seized and were dissolved, but I.G. Farben was
simply too big and too successful to die. And so it was
not killed off completely. Some of I.G. Farben's assets
were seized by the US authorities, but a large part of
the business was simply restructured. Instead of being

killed, it was rebranded and its assets split across several new entities, including the big name brands Agfa, BASF, Bayer and Sanofi. This meant that many of the key managerial personnel and employees kept similar jobs doing similar things. For all intents and purposes, I.G. Farben survived the war, albeit in a range of different guises with their own corporate personalities.

Those brands are now recognised as household-name chemical companies, as the manufacturers of audio tapes and CDs, film, camera equipment, medicines and so on. There is no doubt that since World War II those brands have played a significant role in the development of the German and the global economy. And this is the reason I.G. Farben was kept alive, in its different guises, to ensure that the power of German capital could be harnessed after the political regime had been toppled. The purpose of keeping the I.G. Farben companies alive was to help maintain a healthy environment for German and international investors.

Given their history, we are impelled to wonder what happened to those companies next, and, in particular, whether they have managed to shake off their legacy. The answer is not exactly clear, yet there have certainly been some questionable activities linked to I.G. Farben companies since World War II. BASF has been named *the* "environmental bad boy in China"[5] by Greenpeace because of its failure to disclose key information about the development of a mega plant producing highly toxic chemicals. The drug-maker, Sanofi, also has a dubious environmental record. In 2018, the company was forced to close the firm's Mourenx plant in south-west France, which produces the epilepsy treatment Valproate, because investigators discovered air pollut-ants at 7,000 times the limit allowed by French law.[6] Agfa, now part of the Belgian-owned conglomeration Agfa-Gaerhart, is not regarded as a particularly seri-ous environmental offender, but has faced criticism for pollution at some of its sites. One of those is in Shoreham, Long Island, where it operated a photograph processing plant.[7]

Of all the corporations in the I.G. Farben group, it is Bayer that has amassed the worst reputation for its impact on people and the environment. In 2010, Bayer was ranked the worst toxic air polluter in the US by the Political Economy Research Institute at the University of Massachusetts Amerhurst; in 2016, it was ranked third worst.[8] Bayer has faced a number of major crises in relation to the persistent health and environmental impact of its chemicals. It recently lobbied unsuccess-fully to prevent the EU ban on neonicotinoids, the insecticide that was developed by Shell and Bayer in the 1990s and is thought to be threatening bee colonies. It is now facing a major crisis. As the parent company of Monsanto, Bayer has responsibility for compensat-ing the victims of PCB and its Roundup weed killer (both noted in the introduction to this book). After the story of the Roundup cancer claims broke, Bayer CEO Werner Baumann told the press: "If we can settle nuisances at some point where the defense costs in preparing cases are higher than potential settlement amounts, we will of course consider it from an economic standpoint".[9] Baumann's statement reflects two basic truths about the corporate economy. First, claims by victims are "nuisances", mere inconveniences to the more important task of getting on with business. Second, corporate decisions, even life and death decisions, are taken from an "economic standpoint".

The point being made here is not that Volkswagen or any of the companies that inherited the mantle of I.G. Farben have something residual in their DNA or their own particular legacy which gives them a proclivity for genocide or ecocide. The point is rather more mundane: that corporations will use their gift of immortality in ways that harm the environment or even kill and maim human beings as long as the economics make sense.

Stora Enso is now embroiled in a series of struggles with local people in Brazil and Uruguay who claim that its forest plantations are violating basic environmental principles, depleting water sources and destroying the biodiversity of huge areas of land. According to Amigos de la Tierra España (ATE part of Friends of the Earth International), the company has had a devastating effect on the rainforests. Its use of huge swathes of forestry in Uruguay and Brazil has led to sustained conflicts with the landless peasant movement. ATE have noted:

> In South America, Stora Enso drives an aggressive expansion strategy, increasing its industrial capacity and the area covered in eucalyptus plantations for

cellulose production. The expansion of tree monocultures threatens highly biodiverse ecosystems such as Atlantic Forest, the "Cerrado" savannah and "Pampa" grassland and fundamentally changes the socio-productive structures of the region".[10]

The chilling question the Stora story raises is this: will corporations still formally be in existence after the Atlantic Forest has disappeared? Will they still be irreversibly damaging the environment after the traditional land-owning communities have left the Cerrado savannah and Pampa grassland? If the history of this corporation and of the corporate economy is anything to go by, a safe answer would be, yes. Unless we do something to change things, corporations are capable of keeping on going after the living environment around them has been destroyed and the last human being has been evicted.

We will return to the Stora story in the next chapter. For the moment, it is enough to say that this is a story, just like the Volkswagen and the I.G. Farben/Bayer stories, that forces us to ask a basic question: how can we have created an "immortal" being that makes life and death decisions not from a human standpoint, but from an "economic standpoint"? It is this question that the rest of this chapter sets out to answer.

A very peculiar "person"

There are endless debates in law journals, in business schools and in the economics departments of universities that have produced pile upon pile of books and articles on corporate theory. Those academic tracts seek to explain how and why the corporation has been created in a particular form. Many of those tracts debate the merits of the "corporate person", both in theory and practice. This chapter will not try to capture the full complexity of the evolution of the corporate person or resolve any of those debates. Its purpose is much more modest: simply to give an introduction to the historical development of the most influential theories of the corporation in order to provide a framework for understanding what the corporation is. By doing so, we get closer to understanding why the corporation apparently has an in-built propensity to destroy the natural environment. A crash course in corporate legal theory is probably not what you agreed to when you picked up this book. And, no matter how accessibly written it may be, theory is never an easy read. But we need to have a basic understanding of theory in order to grasp exactly how and why the corporation has ecocidal tendencies. The discussion that follows explains the key theoretical concepts that have shaped the peculiar immortal being that we call the corporation.

For social theorists like Zygmunt Bauman, the author of *Modernity and the Holocaust*,[11] human tragedies are made possible by the *structure* of the modern system of government itself. Bauman analysed the Nazi holocaust in an attempt to understand how one group of human beings were capable of the genocide of another group of human beings. The idea of distance and space was crucial to Bauman in his analysis. He argued that the bureaucratic structure of states is profoundly *dehumanising*. Elements of this dehumanising structure which made the holocaust possible include a highly instrumental rationality guiding the organisation, obedience to a rigidly enforced set of rules, and a division of labour based on smaller and smaller tasks. The multiple layers of rigidly enforced decisions in modern bureaucracies create physical and moral distance between those who take decisions to do something and those who then execute the decisions. Bureaucratic structures can therefore physically and ontologically remove the perpetrators from even the most extreme acts of violence; the various decisions and actions taken by different elements of the bureaucracy enable extreme acts of violence to be normalised. The corporation works in precisely the same way. Indeed, as this chapter will show, it is the same set of structural dynamics within corporations that provide the foundations of the corporation's *dehumanising* force and it is through the creation of the corporate person that the corporation's capacity to act in an anti-human way is critically enhanced.

Most of the earliest forms of corporation were not based on a very developed notion of "personhood". Indeed, in most European countries "incorporations" were established by some form of royal charter or act of parliament. Up to the mid-nineteenth century, most corporations were granted specific powers to do specific things by their charter. It was through legal theory, mainly written by the leading judges of the time, that the corporation began to adopt the characteristics of the corporate person.

George MacKenzie's *Law and Customs of Scotland in Matters Criminal*, published in 1678, outlined the basis for how an "incorporation" can be regarded in law as a legal subject. Incorporations, he argued, could even be held guilty of a crime:

> "Even these Crymes which are ordinarly committed by privat men, such as Murder, Oppression, etc. are in Law sometimes charged upon the Incorporations; if these things be done by command of the Rulers".[12]

In modern parlance, MacKenzie's argument suggests that the crimes committed as a result of decisions taken by a single owner, a board of directors or by senior management can be imputed to the corporate person and the latter could therefore be indicted for those crimes, just as individual "rulers" could.

The idea of the corporate person was developed and shaped by an endless trail of legal tracts like MacKenzie's in Europe and North America between the seventeenth and nineteenth centuries. Those various academic works and legal tracts that influenced the development of the *concept* of corporate person are collectively known as "fictional" or "artificial" entity theory.[13] This concept describes how the corporation is artificially constructed as a fictional, as opposed to real, flesh and blood, person. The corporate person is able to conduct commercial functions as if it was a real person. It is permitted to enter into commercial agreements as a contracting party. In short, the status of the corporation in law is analogous to the sole proprietor of a business.

The fictional entity approach used a logic that led to the corporation being understood as a "person" in a whole range of new ways. In the UK, a series of important cases asserted the idea that the corporate person rather than the shareholder must be regarded as the owner of assets and property. Shareholders' assets could therefore be protected from losses accrued by the companies they owned or held shares in, even in very small, family-run businesses. In the US, a series of cases that spanned the nineteenth century sought court rulings on the "citizenship" claims of corporate persons: could corporations be regarded in law as having equal status to human citizens? The answer was, for the most part, yes.[14] In the nineteenth century, it became obvious that the fictional entity had outgrown the original intention of its designers. A combination of decisions made in those cases, alongside legislation that was being introduced in many industrialised states, meant that the corporation had become a *general* rather than a *specific* form of organisation. No longer would governments issue a charter for a specific purpose. Now corporate law enabled corporations to be formed for *any* purpose. The full consequences of this move from the specific to the general form of organisation will be explored in the following chapter.

Another changing feature of the corporation was to have a profound influence on the development of the theory and practice of corporate law. Until the colonial period, almost all charters were issued to non-profit organisations. As a commercial entity that had been granted a charter, Stora Kopparberg would have been a relatively rare type of organisation in Europe before the end of the sixteenth century. However, as the corporation developed as a major site of *capitalist* investment, commercial law also played a central role in shaping the rules that corporations had to follow. The evolution of the corporation into a profit-making organisation meant that it also had to be governed by commercial law, in particular, by the sections of commercial law known as "contract law".

"Contractual" theories (sometimes known in different variations as "aggregate", "agency" or "nexus of contract" theory) see the corporation as a natural extension to the market. The corporation is viewed as a private arena that functions to enhance commercial transactions between individuals; and it should be understood not as a singular entity, but as a nexus of contracts between different individuals that make up the corporation.

Most of the books and articles that have analysed the theories of the corporation have stressed the contradictions between fictional entity theory and contractual theory.[15] Yet, in practice, the law has evolved in a way that enables both approaches to shape the foundations of the corporation's legal authority.

The corporate person (the fictional entity) is made compatible with contract theory precisely because in virtually all aspects of what the corporation does, it is the corporate person that is the principle contracting party. It is generally the corporate person that purchases land, is granted a licence to extract resources, to manufacture and buy and sell things. In this sense, the corporate person is the most important legal subject in commercial activities involving the corporation; it is the corporate person rather than any individual director or investor that is the primary contracting party in virtually all of those transactions with external parties. When it comes to contracts *inside* the corporation, the corporate person is an equally important contracting party. Workers are employed by the corporate person; the key relationships in franchise arrangements, supply chains and in subsidiary/parent relationships are between different corporate persons, each acting as a contracting party.

If most of the business of the corporation involves the corporate person as the responsible contracting party, there is one contractual relationship that exists between different human constituents within this corporation. This is the relationship between the executives of the corporation and the corporation's owners or investors. It is a relationship that many contractual theorists agree is more important than any other inside the corporation.[16] They have a point. In law, this relationship takes priority over all others. We will return to the significance of this relationship later in the chapter. For the time being, we simply note that contract law has effectively consolidated corporate personhood and extended the role of corporations as entities with rights and responsibilities that are similar to real persons. This, as the next section will show, has created some deep contradictions in law.

The "rights" of the corporate person

As we have seen, the corporation could, in theory, be understood as a "citizen" and held criminally responsible for its actions. The same development of the idea of the corporate person in law also meant that the corporation could conceivably have "rights" as a legal subject.

Infamously, the "rights" of the corporation have been underpinned by the US constitution. The 14th Amendment to the US constitution asserts that government cannot "deprive any person of life, liberty or property, without due process of law; nor deny to any person within its jurisdiction the equal protection of the laws". A claim over improper tax assessment that came to the court in 1886 set an important precedent. In a headnote to the case that subsequently became much more important than the substance of the ruling itself, Chief Justice Morrison Waite stated:

> The Court does not wish to hear argument on the question whether the provision in the Fourteenth Amendment to the Constitution, which forbids a state to deny to any person within its jurisdiction the equal protection of the laws, applies to these corporations. We are all of the opinion that it does.[17]

The rest is corporate history. Corporations have invoked their rights in a string of cases over the years, and this reasoning has bled into human rights law. Although it is not universally applied, in many jurisdictions, corporate personhood enables corporations to seek redress in law for human rights violations against them.[18] Access to a range of other court and tribunal mechanisms can be used strategically by corporations to assert "rights" in cases against government interference.[19] Needless to say, this is a matter of some controversy and provoked a public campaign following the Citizens United case heard at the US Supreme Court in 2010.[20] In this case, the court ruled that corporations have the right to spend money supporting candidates in elections, and may, on religious grounds, refuse to comply with a federal mandate to cover birth control in their employee health plans. The court ruled that a corporation has the right to religious observance!

Since the 1950s, the legal status of corporations has also been protected in European human rights law. Article 1 Protocol 1 of the European Convention on Human Rights (ECHR)[21] reads: "Every natural or legal person is entitled to the peaceful enjoyment of his possessions". The wording is deliberate: the inclusion of legal persons means corporate persons are protected by the ECHR. The volume of cases in which corporations claim human rights is not insignificant. Indeed, one study has estimated that 4% of cases in the European Court of Human Rights are applications filed by companies or other legal persons pursuing corporate interests.[22]

Most of the cases in which corporations have the protection of the European Court of Human Rights have been for alleged violations of property rights, the right to a fair trial and, in some cases, freedom of expression. In many of those cases, the human rights issue revolves around overly invasive or burdensome regulatory requirements or state investigations.[23] In other words human rights protections are used to neutralise attempts by states to protect the public.

In international law the fictional entity and the contractual approach combine powerfully to grant the corporate person rights that vastly enhance its contractual power. For example, bi-lateral and multi-lateral trade agreements between nations typically include guarantees of access to particular markets for foreign investors. If access to those markets is not forthcoming, or is prevented in some way, corporations have the right to "sue" governments as part of an Investor State Dispute Settlement (ISDS) process, with a case normally heard in an international court. Those ISDS mechanisms enable corporations to challenge states' infringement of their "rights" enshrined in trade agreements.

Very often ecosystems are at stake in such cases. Indeed, one analysis of cases heard at the most frequently used forum for those cases (the International Center for Settlement of Investment Disputes) shows that a total of 60 out of 169 (or 37%) of cases relate to the oil, gas or mining industries.[24] Quebec has been prevented from banning fracking and the EU prevented from banning the import of high carbon oil from Alberta tar sands using the same procedure.[25] Moreover, the proportion of cases relating to health, environmental, energy, toxics, financial, land-use or other regulatory policies is now growing.[26] As journalist Michael Parenti notes:

> Under the free trade accords, corporate investment rights have been upraised to imperial supremacy, able to take precedent over all other rights, including the right to a clean, livable environment, the right to affordable public services, and the right to any morsel of political-economic democracy.[27]

Over a period of 30 years, ChevronTexaco did untold damage to human populations and to the ecosystem on the Lago Agrio oil fields in Ecuador. A civil action against ChevronTexaco for its destruction of the environment saw the Ecuador Supreme Court order compensation of $US 9.5 million. The corporation successfully sued the Ecuador government at the International Arbitration Tribunal in The Hague under the Bilateral Investment Treaty. The Tribunal ordered that the Ecuadorian government annul the sentence issued by its courts.[28]

ChevronTexaco have been accused of wiping out entire tribes. Oil extraction in the Amazon in some places has led to irrevocable damage to food and water supplies, the introduction of new diseases, and ultimately the extinction of entire tribes. Some have called this *cultural* genocide. Others drop the word "cultural" and call it plain *genocide*. As the journalist Kerry Kennedy has reported:

Texaco knew people would die because of what they were doing, and they ignored it. At last count, 1,400 children, women, and men have died of illnesses directly attributed to Texaco's contamination. Cancer rates in communities affected by oil activity are 30 times higher than anywhere else in the country. Other medical teams have documented elevated rates of birth defects, miscarriages, skin disease, and nerve damage. Two nomadic groups that once inhabited the region, the Tetetes and the Sansahuari, have been wiped out.[29]

This evidence is supported by extensive academic research and reports by prominent non-governmental organisations (NGOs).[30] And yet, in the end, it was the Ecuadorean government that had to step back from demanding any payment for the damages. ChevronTexaco is by no means alone in facing such allegations. In the Amazon in Northern Peru, the Canadian oil company Talisman was charged by Peru's Public Ministry with "attempted genocide" in 2014 for provoking a standoff with the Achuar people of the Pastaza River Basin over rights to their land.[31]

Therein lies a rather stark contradiction in law: although corporations can be protected by human rights law, they can at the same time enjoy impunity for committing human rights violations and for committing environmental atrocities, even genocide. It is clear from those cases and countless others in Asia, Latin America, Africa and Australia, in which corporate human rights violations are alleged,[32] that people are being legally dispossessed of their ancestral land by corporations,[33] and corporations are colluding with death squads to commit human rights violations with impunity.[34] In many cases, corporations are permitted to poison air and water supplies and destroy bio-diverse areas because we have an international legal system that now privileges corporate rights above the future of the planet and its people.[35] When we scrutinise this system, it reveals the close connection between this concept of the corporate person and the destruction of the planet.

Externalising the costs of environmental damage

The use of contract law as the basis for the corporation's legal authority poses an immediate problem for controlling environmental harm. The question of whether a corporation should be made to pay for environmental crimes on the scale of ChevronTexaco's cultural genocide is very often reduced to an argument over its responsibilities as a contracting party. This is because the consequences of corporate activity for the environment are generally not included in commercial contracts.

The term *externalities* is used to describe the social and environmental harms caused by corporations that are never fully accounted for in contracts. The costs that *are* typically counted are the standard inputs of commercial or productive activity: the costs of raw materials, of processing these through energy and using technologies, the costs of building or renting and maintaining premises and the costs of labour. The costs to communities resulting from environmental damage, or to workers due to industrial diseases and injuries are not a contractual matter and therefore do not appear in a company's annual accounts simply because, more often than not, corporations will not have to pay those costs. Related costs may be counted if, for example, civil proceedings have been made to recover them, or there is a criminal/regulatory fine to pay. They may also be indirectly costed in the form of an insurance premium. However, the bulk of those costs are borne by individuals (e.g. loss of earnings to a family when someone is made ill by industrial activity) or they are socialised (and borne by tax payers through public health systems and subsidies.

At the same time, environmental pollution caused by corporations tends to have the biggest impact on people that do not have any contract with the corporation. They are "non-contracting parties". Communities affected by pollution, for example, will not have a contract with the corporation. They may be protected by regulations that are upheld by the state, and some versions of corporate aggregate theory would define such relationships as "contractual". Yet those communities are never granted the same rights as *formal* contract holders. Despite recent campaigns that seek rights to be granted directly to natural resources, a lake or a river cannot have a contract with a corporation that protects it against pollution in any meaningful sense.[36]

Indeed, many of the costs of corporate activity that are not recognised in contract right now *can* be counted and accounted for. The health problems associated with the deadly substances discussed in the introduction to this book can all be costed. We can estimate the medical and other economic costs borne by those who are made ill by particulate pollution, by lead in petrol, by polyvinyl chloride compounds, by asbestos and so on. We can even estimate some of the environmental costs. The main reason they are excluded is not because they cannot be counted, but because they are rendered invisible by normal accounting and contracting practice; they remain externalities. Changing contracting and accounting practice would be a step forward, but it would not necessarily offer a transformative solution. Often, there are costs to the environment created by chemicals and by the carbon economy which are so great they could and should never be reduced to a financial number. How could we put a figure on the global climate crisis? Far less, apportion costs to each corporation?

When we examine the system of accounting for environmental costs, we see how it is weighed heavily in the favour of the corporation. The full costs will never be borne by the corporate person since the system is set up to ensure that they will be borne by real persons.

There are ways in which the costs of externalities can be *re-internalised* indirectly through legal redress. So, for example, if a corporation is successfully sued by a community for environmental damage, the effect is that some of those costs are reinternalised, bringing the responsibility for bearing them back inside the corporation. Of course, the courts are not always able to calculate the damage of a chemical company or incinerator to the environment in economic terms. Those costs are often unmeasurable.

However, even when a modest attempt to recover some costs is made by victims and by communities the corporate person comes to the rescue. In cases where the costs of externalities might be re-internalised in the ways set out above, the fictional entity of the corporation allows the impact of such legal action to be minimised. This is sometimes achieved through the establishment of complex corporate chains of ownership. Corporate personhood allows a partition to be drawn between different corporate entities. When a corporation establishes a subsidiary or a parent company, it effectively extends the ownership structure of the corporation. A parent or holding company can be created in order to "own" the company, and a subsidiary can be created to own a specific part of the company, or own particular assets. The corporation can therefore create its own complex world of ownership relationships. In other words, each of those relationships is protected by a corporate veil.

This is how it works. A corporation can create a multitude of different persons, each with their own identity and entity status (by establishing a chain of subsidiaries or sister firms) and multiple nationalities (by basing themselves in several different countries simultaneously). Corporations can therefore act in the name of a multitude of split personalities that enables them to diversify their assets across any number of different identities and locations. The advantages of multiple- and split-corporate personhood extend into everything the corporation does. Take, for example, what happens when a corporate person rather than a real person is regarded as an employer. When the corporation is the employer, the owners of the corporation, or the share-holders, cannot be held directly responsible for any liabilities that arise from the labour relationship; nor will they have any obligation to know about, far less do anything about, the labour conditions faced by workers in any of the companies that they own or invest in. When a company uses subsidiaries to employ workers, it becomes even easier for both individual shareholders and executives to avoid responsibility for subsidiar-ies' unfair labour practices or for discrimination and other nefarious practices. And when this happens on an international scale, multinational and transnational corporations are very often able to make it impossible to see clearly who owes liabilities to workers or com-munities. Sometimes this multi-national or transna-tional structure prevents compensation being paid by a parent company when a harm is caused by a local subsidiary.[37]

Ownership relationships can be manipulated years after any incident or problem occurs. In the case of what may be the worst single environmental disas-ter in history, this is exactly what is going on. The company responsible for the 1984 Bhopal chemical leaks in India, which killed 20,000–30,000 people, was

Union Carbide. In the decade and a half that followed the disaster, Union Carbide paid minimal compensation, which was wholly inadequate for dealing with the clean-up and the medical costs to victims, and in any case was only partially distributed.[38] In February 2001, Dow acquired all of the shares of Union Carbide, meaning that the corporation became a wholly owned subsidiary of Dow. Since then, Dow has denied all liabilities in the legal actions initiated by victims, because, it claims "Under well-established principles of corporate law, both in India and the US, TDCC did not assume UCC's liabilities as part of the 2001 transaction".[39] So far, Dow's argument has been successful in the US courts. Union Carbide retained the same basic structure, management and scope of activities; the only difference is in the ownership structure. But this ownership structure has been enough to effectively indemnify both senior managers and investors for the horror caused by Union Carbide. More than 120,000 people still suffer from medical conditions, some in constant pain, because of the leak and the subsequent pollution of the surrounding area.[40]

Externalising legal liability

Corporate personhood poses a distinct problem for controlling environmental harm. It allows corporate executives and corporate owners and shareholders to externalise their liabilities for the environmental damage done by the corporation.

Let us consider the way that shareholders are protected from their liabilities first. An invisible corporate veil is drawn not only between different corporate
entities as described above, but also between the corporation and its owners and shareholders. The legal
principle known as *limited liability* is key to understanding how this works. Limited liability is the term
that describes the process used to protect the liabilities
of the owners or investors of a corporation. Because
the corporation is treated in law as a separate person,
it is formally regarded as the owner of all assets. And
because the assets are owned by the corporate person,
the owner or shareholder in a limited company is not
generally held personally liable for what the corporation does with those assets. If the corporation owes
liabilities, then owners or investors cannot lose any
more than the amount they have invested in the company; they are generally not held responsible for the
debts or other liabilities of the company. Neither are
they normally held responsible for the costs of any
legal proceedings that may arise from its activities.[41]

The principle of "entity shielding" works using
a similar trick, as a kind of limited liability rule in
reverse. Whereas limited liability protects investor's
assets from the corporation's creditors, the principle of
entity shielding ensures that the corporation's assets
cannot be used to pay the liabilities of the owners or
shareholders. In other words, the corporate veil also
protects the *corporate* person from the liabilities of
its owners and investors. One advantage that can be

gained from "entity shielding", therefore, is that the investor can transfer ownership of assets to the corporation to ensure those assets will not be lost in the event of personal bankruptcy.

It is seldom acknowledged by corporate lawyers, but the corporate veil also protects CEOs, senior managers and boards of directors to ensure that the people who lead the corporation and who are the key decision-makers are held not personally liable when things go wrong. A clear example of this is the financial crisis of 2008. There is more than enough evidence to convict a large number of individuals in the US finance industry for a range of serious frauds that caused the 2008 financial crash.[42] Yet the crisis prompted hardly any investigations or prosecutions of individuals.[43] Criminologist Greg Barak noted in 2012 that "No senior executives from any of the major financial institutions had been criminally charged, prosecuted, or imprisoned".[44] One trader, Kareem Serageldin, who worked for Credit Suisse, did serve a sentence for inflating the value of mortgage bonds in his trading portfolio.[45]

There have been a number of executives prosecuted for the fraudulent use of bailout money after the crisis, and this is important to recognise. Yet most of these cases involved people working for small-time community and regional banks. As the *New York Times* noted: "prominent Wall Street executives have escaped largely unscathed".[46] The most prominent and powerful executives have been protected precisely because illegal practices in banking and finance have mainly targeted the *corporate* person. In May 2018, the total fine imposed on the Royal Bank of Scotland (RBS) for offences related to the 2008 crash totalled over $10 billion. This came on the back of similarly large fines levied on US and European banks.[47] In most areas of corporate regulation, the vast majority of prosecutions put corporations rather than individuals in the dock, especially when it comes to corporate environmental and safety violations. Around 3% of prosecutions for health and safety offences are filed against directors or senior managers; 95% are against corporate persons.[48] When it comes to environmental offences, directors and senior managers are penalised in only the rarest cases, and it is normally only in the smallest companies that those individuals face punishment. Again, the vast majority of environmental prosecutions are filed against corporate persons.[49]

The corporation's structural architecture ensures that corporate owners and investors, and directors and senior managers, will almost always be protected from liability, no matter what the corporation does. Legal action against the corporate person is unlikely to be effective precisely for this reason: the corporate veil ensures that legal intervention will only very rarely touch the people who cause environmental harms and those that stand to profit the most. We are therefore locked in a paradox: if we argue for more *corporate* punishment then we simultaneously argue for the impunity of the people who stand behind the corporate veil. Yet, if we argue for softer or less punitive forms of intervention, then we merely legitimise the damage done to the environment by corporations.

Director vs corporate responsibility

In 1910 a British diplomat, Roger Casement, discovered a series of horrific atrocities committed by a British rubber corporation, the Peruvian Amazon Company in the Putumayo region of the Amazon rainforest. His subsequent reports to the British government made visible the murder and terror suffered by indigenous peoples who were forced to work for the Peruvian Amazon Company. *The New York Times* reported Casement's findings, noting that the crimes he discovered:

> included innumerable murders and torture of defenseless Indians, pouring kerosene oil over men and then setting fire to them, burning them at the stake, dashing out the brains of children, and again cutting off the arms and legs of Indians and leaving them to speedy death in their agony.[50]

The Putomayo case opened a public debate about corporate accountability. It was openly acknowledged by government and the business world that the relative autonomy of the corporation's employees from its investors had effectively enabled the continuation of British slavery in Peru. Indeed, Casement's report had pointed out that the crimes of the Peruvian Amazon Company arose directly as a result of the structure of the modern corporation. The corporation had created a method for investors to extract profits without any need to know or care about the human consequences.

> To get rich quick ... by the crushing enslavement of a hapless subject people – this is the explanation ... The rubber was there. How it was produced, out of what hell of human suffering no one knew, no one asked, so one suspected. Can it be no one cared?[51]

A House of Commons Select Committee considered Casement's evidence. It stopped short of pointing the finger at investors, but highlighted the criminality of the corporation's directors. It concluded that although the directors could plausibly claim that they knew little of the atrocities in the Amazon, they were guilty of "culpable negligence".[52]

In the first half of the twentieth century, a number of prominent legal scholars began again to forcefully make the case for a "director primacy model" of the corporation.[53] A series of cases invoking the doctrine of *ultra vires* highlighted the inherent conflict between the fictional or artificial entity and the 'contractual' perspectives. In latin, the phrase *ultra vires* simply means "beyond its powers". In corporate law, the *ultra vires* doctrine is based on a recognition that a corporation can only legitimately do things that are within the scope of its charter, its articles of incorporation or other founding documents.

The so-called *ultra vires* cases, mainly initiated in the US and UK courts, therefore centred around the scope of what a corporation was or was not permitted to do. The legal argument that was accepted in a number of key court cases proceeded along the following lines: if the corporation did things that are beyond the scope of its charter, then those things could be considered void or exempt from legal proceedings, since the corporation was acting beyond its mandate. The problem for the courts was that the corporate person in those cases was being used in ways that undermined business relationships. If contracts could be so easily invalidated, would this not limit risk taking and entrepreneurialism? One scholar, A.L. Goodhart, convincingly argued in the pages of the *Cambridge Law Journal* in 1926 that the only plausible way to respond to this dilemma, and at the same time avoid piercing the veil that protected shareholders and investors, was to change the law and allow directors who had authorised the *ultra vires* contract to be held legally responsible.

Similar arguments had been developing in legal theories proposed by academics throughout the twentieth century. A number of theorists, led by the German legal historian Otto Gierke,[54] set out to show that if investors or directors were not to be held fully liable for damages incurred to workers, communities or other parties, or indeed for their crimes, then *corporations* should be. This approach, known later as "real entity theory" was in essence a response to the glaring gaps in accountability that corporate law was opening up.[55] The reasoning those scholars followed was a historical one. They pointed out that because we find political and even legal notions of a collective identity of the "corporation" in the middle ages, there is therefore a deep historical precedent for understanding corporations as having an identity in the fullest possible legal sense.[56]

Real entity theory regards the corporation as an autonomous actor, separate from the shareholders, managers and other significant groups of individuals that comprise the corporation. And because of this, the line of argument follows, the corporation is understood as having the capacity to act as an independent decision-maker. Thinkers like British socialist politician and legal scholar Harold Laski promoted the real entity model because they thought that if carefully regulated and not left to its own devices, the corporation could be a force for social good. In many ways, this formulation was a crucial forerunner to more recent demands for corporate social responsibility. Laski proposed that if the corporation can act as a collective, social entity, not as a purely political one (as proposed by fictional entity theory) or as an economic one (as proposed by contractual theory), then it can potentially act responsibly. In 1932, US legal theorist Merrick Dodd formulated a real entity theory argument for the restructuring of corporate goals that proposed "director primacy" rather than shareholder primacy:

> If the unity of the corporate body is real, then there is reality and not simply legal fiction in the proposition that the managers of the unit are fiduciaries for *it and not merely for its individual members*, that they are ... trustees for an institution rather than attorneys for the stockholders. ... A sense of social responsibility toward

employees, consumers, and the general public may thus come to be regarded as the appropriate attitude to be adopted by those who are engaged in business.[57]

Dodd and the real entity theorists argued that the growing power that directors enjoyed as the "controllers" of the corporation could be harnessed for good by extending their legal duties to other stakeholders, like employees and local communities.

Shareholder primacy

But the commentators and legal scholars who wanted to make corporate executives directly responsible were struggling in rapid currents of legal opinion that flowed in the opposite direction. At the beginning of the twentieth century, contractual theories of the corporation were being asserted in key cases. In particular, the courts were being asked to rule on the question of the duties owed by directors to shareholders and to broader social interests. The US case *Dodge vs Ford Motor Company*[58] was perhaps the most influential case to assert that the primary responsibility of the executives is to act in the interests of its shareholders, rather than its employees, customers or the wider community. In the Dodge case, two of the largest shareholders objected to the way that Henry Ford was channelling the profits of the company. He sought to divert cash that would previously have been given to shareholders in dividends to pay for investment in new plants that would enable Ford to dramatically increase production. The Michigan Supreme Court ruling prohibited Henry Ford from lowering consumer prices and raising employee salaries. This is the principle known as "shareholder primacy" in Anglo-American corporate law. I say "Anglo-American", since in many other national jurisdictions, like Japan and Germany, corporate law allows for a wider consideration of the different stakeholders involved in business, and therefore allows for a much wider understanding of how the "success" of the company might be measured.[59]

Today, the Dodge decision looks extremely dogmatic in places that are influenced by the Anglo-American model of corporate law. Since at least the 1960s, the courts in the US – and indeed most other jurisdictions – have explicitly recognised that directors can exercise more expansive judgement and can make decisions if they are clearly made to benefit the corporation as a whole. Since the Dodge decision, there has been a high degree of legal and political convergence around the principle of shareholder primacy even in jurisdictions with a different approach like Germany and Japan. The legal basis of the principle of shareholder primacy has been challenged.[60] Yet it has become, in practice, the single most important guiding principle in defining where power lies in corporations. While directors have some discretion to pursue policies that might benefit other groups (workers, consumers and so on), they can only do so if such policies can, in the final reckoning, be regarded as being in the interests of shareholders.[61] The way the law establishes executives' and directors' fiduciary responsibilities[62] ensures that their discretion to take decisions is ultimately limited by their primary duty to ensure the success of the corporation, a duty that is normally interpreted as acting on behalf of shareholders.[63]

The principle of shareholder primacy was underlined in what is probably the most influential text ever written on the corporation. In 1932, US diplomat Adolf Berle and economist Gardiner Means published *The Modern Corporation and Private Property*. The book assembled empirical evidence to show how, by the beginning of the twentieth century, we had begun to see within corporations a clear (formal) separation of ownership and control, whereby owners of the business and shareholders were no longer expected to manage the day-to-day affairs of the business. The day of the factory master who owned both a significant part of the business, and at the same time oversaw the running of the factory, was over; by the beginning of the twentieth century, the majority of shareholders of any given corporation were not generally involved with operational decision-making in the corporations they had a stake in.[64] This severing of owners from the management of the corporation released the investor from any clear line of responsibility for the corporation's actions. Berle and Means' proposal that the distancing of investors from corporate activity might lead the corporation to "serve not alone the owners or the control, but all society" today sounds somewhat naive.[65]

Powerful arguments to hold directors accountable

for corporate wrongdoing never went away, but they were carefully circumscribed by the principle of shareholder primacy in the development of legislation and case law through the twentieth century. If there was one thing that the most prominent corporate theorists and the law courts agreed on, it was that directors owed an immeasurably greater duty to investors than they did to communities or workers, or even their customers and suppliers.

Structures of irresponsibility

The corporate structure, as it became enshrined in law in the twentieth century, insisted that managers focus on one responsibility above all others: shareholder value. This is not to say that all decisions at all times are based upon short-term profitability. Far from it; often more strategic managements do pursue interests that are more long-term, that stabilise the corporation's relationship with a range of different communities, and which combine its responsibilities to different stakeholders. The effect of the principle of shareholder primacy is much more subtle and insidious. It allows directors to choose to remain distant from the real conditions of production; it allows lines of accountability for decisions to be blurred, and ultimately eradicates the incentives necessary to be "responsible" to anyone else. As sociologist Frank Pearce has argued in his powerful analysis of corporate rationality, the dominant features of the formal organisation of the corporation combine to produce "structures of irresponsibility".[66] Some of those features are familiar by now (the fiduciary duties of directors to maximise profits for a distant constituency of shareholders and the rules of incorporation that grant it a range of structural advantages related to the corporate veil). Others will be developed in the coming chapters (its autocratic and strictly hierarchical command structure and its tightly constructed profit-oriented goals).

It is through the dominant values of the organisation (profit orientation, shareholder value and so on) that the formal separation of the various elements of the corporations are organised in a hierarchical way. As we have seen, investors' interests are placed above the interests of managers, who have very clearly defined powers over other employees. Some of the early real entity theorists realised that the "value of corporate privilege depends upon the separation of capacities"[67] within corporations.

The separation of the corporation's capacities is realised through the physical separation of the different human constituents of the corporate person (investors, lenders, creditors, owners, directors, managers and workers). Just like Zygmunt Bauman's description of the profoundly dehumanising character of bureaucratic structures, the corporation allows its human constituents to remain indifferent to the social and human impact of production processes and investment strategies. Investors and corporate executives are both physically distanced and legally protected from the consequences of corporate activities. They can therefore remain focussed on profitability without ever having to see or know about the human consequences of their decisions. Given this combination of incentives, impunity and fractured division of function, it is indeed difficult to see how corporations could *ever* act responsibly.

It is this formal separation of roles within a tightly organised hierarchy that makes the corporation anti-social and anti-human. Shareholders are remote and often have a large number of diverse investments across different corporations. The corporation developed in this way, not merely as a matter of historical coincidence, or a twist of fate. The corporation is structured in this way precisely to enable a system of investment that is dehumanised. It evolved as a mechanism that would allow investors to pursue their "economic standpoint" above any other standpoint. And to fully understand this, we need to understand how the corporation was synonymous with a process of *financialisation*.

Indeed, the rise of the corporation to dominance in industrialising economies in the nineteenth and twentieth centuries is itself essentially a process of financialisation. By this, I mean that it is based on the promotion of "financial motives, financial markets, financial actors and financial institutions"[68] in the economy. This is what the corporation does. It creates a management structure and investment structure that are formally kept separate in ways that prioritise the investor's interest regardless of the human consequences. But it does this in a very particular way. As legal historian Paddy Ireland shows in detail, throughout the nineteenth century, the corporation was gradually "emptied of its human content".[69] The trick that the corporation achieved was to simultaneously ensure that the position of the investor (whether it was a sole owner or a shareholder) was protected *within* the corporation, while at the same time formally rendering the shareholder as a party that existed *outside* the structure of the corporation. The corporation had to be cleansed of people. In a key case in the UK in 1854 (Watson v Spratley), the court determined, in the case of an unincorporated mining company, that shares were to be understood as interests "only in profits". This case was a key development in the shift to sever the share itself from the company; shares became established as an entirely separate form of property, one that provided entitlement to the profits or the financial surplus of a company, rather than its productive capacity or the preservation of its assets in the long-term. As shares became understood as a distinct form of property, this meant that shareholders effectively established two degrees of separation from the company.

The consequence of this process of financialisation, then, is that capitalist social relationships are completely depersonalised, since "persons cease to relate to persons except through the ownership and exchange of things".[70] Indeed, as Ireland noted, the rise of the share as a form of property reflects a more general shift in the nature of property that has taken place over the past 200 years or so, whereby financial capital is increasingly severed from the material basis of productive capital.[71] By the end of the nineteenth century the corporation had become a pure form of finance capital, a form of property in which human decision-making, human logic and human relationships were replaced by financial decisions, financial logics and financial relationships.

Critics of the corporation who place their hope in reforming governance structures, or in demanding that the corporation is made more responsible, fundamentally underestimate how this process of financialisation removes any possibility for corporate social responsibility. In 2010 both BP and Shell faced shareholder rebellions over their plans to develop Canadian tar sands.[72] A close look at the debates that took place between investors prior to each of the company's annual general meetings reveals that they proceeded using a financial, not a social, logic. The institutional investors objecting to tar sands investments did so on the basis that this activity was likely to be fiercely opposed by climate protestors and NGOs, and would therefore involve significant reputational damage. Shareholders' objections were therefore made on the basis that BP and Shell had not shown investors that this activity could actually be profitable. On this basis, it is difficult to disentangle a concept of "responsibility" from the principle of maximising profits for shareholders.[73]

Even where corporate social responsibility is made law, the law tends to leave the underlying structure of power unchallenged. When the UK Companies Act 2006 sought to reform the fiduciary duties of directors to take account of other stakeholders, it did precisely this. The Act sought to impose a modified version of directors' duties: "enlightened shareholder value". The "enlightened" bit referred to the claims which accompanied the legislation: that it would enable a "stakeholders" approach that rejected the exclusivity of shareholders interests and stressed the long-term success of the company as dependent on safeguarding the interests of a range of stakeholders.[74] It promised a genuinely pluralist approach to stakeholders' interests that permitted shareholders' interests to be subordinated to other stakeholders.[75] In order to achieve this, the key section of the Act was the duty to "promote the success of the company for the benefit of its members as a whole". The rest of section 172 brings into play the "need to foster the *company's* business relationships with suppliers, customers and others; the impact of the *company's* operations on the community and the environment and the desirability of the *company* maintaining a reputation for high standards of business conduct". The method the Act used to achieve this upholds the corporate veil by placing duties on directors to act through the "company". Extending powers through the "company" means very little, since "promotion of the success of the company" is, as we have seen, based on the principle of shareholder primacy. And this is how the law can claim to be on the side of all stakeholders, while ensuring that the *status quo* is protected.

It is a *status quo* that ensures both investors and managers remain distant from the real conditions of production, blurs lines of accountability for decisions, and ultimately eradicates the incentives necessary to remain law-abiding. The same structure makes it virtually impossible to hold individuals within the corporation accountable in any meaningful sense. The corporation's core purpose is realised in the transformation of social relationships into financial relationships.

Conclusion: ecocide and the power of elites

It was necessary to explore the key twists and turns in the history of the corporation and the core ideas that shaped its development before we came to understand how it can be described as a structure of irresponsibility. The peculiar concept of corporate personhood was shaped throughout history with one primary purpose in mind: to provide commercial incentives to investors. The corporate person was freed to do this as it gained status as a contracting party and a legal subject in law. The subsequent domination of the principle of shareholder primacy in corporate law is entirely consistent with the development of the corporate 'entity'.

It is by uncovering the theory and practice that

shaped the evolution of the corporation that we begin to understand why, as the introduction to this book noted, the form that the contemporary corporation takes is probably as close as we could get to a model organisation that is capable of destroying the world. The corporation has been created in the image of a "person" that does not have the same responsibilities as you or I, and at the same time enjoys exceptional legal privileges to mask the real ownership of assets, to hide its wealth and to invent any number of other personalities for itself in order to avoid its liabilities. The corporation itself is granted in law a personality that provides impunity to owners; law at the same time enables split corporate personalities to be created; the corporate personality is also used as a legal subject that can be prosecuted and regulated in a way that does not seriously threaten the interests of people that invest in and manage the corporation.

This strange and artificial notion of personality is a crucial concept for understanding the relationship between ecocide and the corporation. As the rest of this book will show, the edifice of the corporation both encourages the destruction of the environment and provides a basis for corporate immunity for those destructive practices. At the same time, real people – investors, shareholders, owners, executives and directors – benefit, vicariously, through the privileges that accrue to the corporate person. If it is often difficult to see who benefits because they are standing behind a multi-layered corporate veil. The most fundamental purpose of the corporation is to reinforce and reproduce the right of the financial elite to accumulate surplus value, in the form of profits, on behalf of "owners", "shareholders" or some other form of rentier.[76] Since at least the end of the nineteenth century, the corporation has been the key institutional mechanism through which surplus value is accrued and then redistributed and re-invested in capitalist social orders. Yet the reproduction of elite power and privilege is rarely seen as the core function of the corporation, even in the most critical of texts and analyses as we shall begin to see in the following chapter.

Ecocide and elite power are therefore two sides of the same coin. The corporation guarantees the reproduction of the elite by any means necessary. Of course, no corporation sets out to destroy the planet. But as the rest of this book will show, the peculiar structure of the corporation makes ecological destruction inevitable. It is a logical outcome of an institution that is designed to dehumanise social relationships and guarantee indifference to human suffering and environmental degradation. The central social and economic role granted to the corporation minimises the chances of any outcome other than the destruction of the natural environment. And, as we shall see in the following chapter, it is the very same dynamic that ensured the corporation was to play a hugely significant part in the history of colonialism.

From colonialism to ecocide: capital's insatiable need to destroy

Stora Enso is one of Uruguay's biggest landowners. It is also a major plantation owner in the Bahia area of Brazil. Let us reflect on this for a moment. If Finland, Stora Enso's home state, was one of Uruguay's biggest landowners then this would have an entirely different meaning. After all, Finland is one European country that never had colonies. And yet Stora Enso has been accused of having a colonial attitude to its operations in both Uruguay and Brazil.

In those countries, Stora Enso has faced criticisms relating to the exploitation of the land and local people, and in Bahia has even been accused of occupying the land illegally.[1] A long struggle with the Brazilian landless peasants' movement (MST) has led to a significant slowing down of production, and even the forced exit of the company from one state, Rio Grande do Sul.[2] In the midst of this struggle, Stora Enso was accused of collusion with the local military to forcibly evict protestors from its plantations.[3]

In its plantations in Uruguay, Brazil and in Asia and Europe what is at stake here is the degree to which

Stora Enso's presence has fundamentally disrupted the ability of local people to live sustainably from the land. Stora Enso claims that its forestry plantations are replenished using a sustainable model, and that it restores trees to areas where there has been deforestation. Local people claim that there is a major difference between Stora Enso's *plantations* and the maintenance of sustainable *forestry*. Those plantations are mainly eucalyptus, a tree that the industry prefers because it is highly productive. Eucalyptus plantations are also notorious for aggressively depleting soil nutrients and lowering water tables. Because they are monocultural and therefore do not adequately replenish the nutrients in the soil, those plantations also depend on high levels of fertiliser, further depleting the land. There are other problems, not least their flammability and propensity to cause forest fires. Similar claims are made about Stora Enso's European operations. They are replacing ancient bio-diverse forests in Lapland, with monocultural tree varieties that are economically efficient but ultimately unsustainable.[4]

One Uruguayan, Flavio Pazos from the World Rainforest Movement, told the corporation's shareholders in 2012:

Stora Enso is destroying not only our land but our future. This company belongs to you. I have the duty to say that you are committing environmental and social crimes all over the World. Just to have more Money. Just to produce more tissue paper. May be your tissue paper is useful to clean your hands. But it won't help you to clean your consciousness.[5]

Yet Stora Enzo, according to its own publicity, is a "renewable materials company", priding itself on its primary purpose of "creating value in a sustainable bioeconomy".[6] Its claim to sustainability, when set against the apparent violence of its alleged land grab and ecological devastation, is a microcosm of the model of European colonial development. The claims transnational corporations[7] make as the guarantors of environmental sustainability contain precisely the same hypocrisy that we find in the classic colonisers' claim to be civilising the savages. In colonial history, civilisation is the precept on which colonial violence was so often based. In the colonial present, environmental sustainability is the precept on which environmental violence is so often based.

The European colonisers' divine project of civilisation was by no means the singular, or even the dominant logic that guided colonialism. As Ellen Meiksins Wood has documented, the most universally applied logic that justified British colonial theft can be found in the work of seventeenth-century liberal political philosopher John Locke. This logic, set out in his *Two Treatises on Government*, intertwined the "civilisation" project with the process of making the land economically productive. And it is the ability to make land productive (measured very crudely in Locke's terms, by profits) that entitles the occupier to ownership of the land.[8] This is the dominant ethical and legal principle that underpinned so much of the European colonial project. Today, it is precisely the same ethical and legal principle that remains dominant in the global economy: economic productiveness comes before local needs and sustainable ways of living. It is a principle that, throughout history, has required a particularly violent and virulent model of capitalist development to realise its goals, a model that, this chapter will argue, would have not been possible without the corporation. As this chapter will show, the corporation was formative in the development of a colonial capitalism that was always ecocidal.

No limits

In the last chapter, we saw how the architecture of the corporation evolved in a very specific way. We saw how the design of this architecture encourages indifference to human suffering and environmental degradation and ensures that social relationships between human beings are reduced to a financial relationship. In so far as it was not fully developed in its current form until the mid-nineteenth century, the invention of the corporation as a convenient institutional mechanism for "capital'"is a comparatively recent one.

By using the term capital, I simply mean wealth in the form of money or other assets that can be traded for money. Capital is normally used either as collateral for credit or can be deposited in a bank or used for some other investment with the purpose of increasing its value. Almost all of the world's capital now flows through some form of corporation. Karl Marx described the motor force of capitalism very clearly in his magnus opus, *Capital*; capitalism entails a never-ending process in which wealth seeks to "reproduce itself". This process cannot happen without people. Behind this process we find two important groups of people with opposing interests: capitalists, who own most of the capital in the form of money and property and who continually seek to expand the value of this capital; and workers, who through their labour, produce "value" in the form of goods and services that capitalists are then able to sell.

Of course, Marx did not write at any length about the corporation *per se*. But he was writing at a time in which the corporate economy had not yet fully developed. He started writing *Capital* roughly around the time the Limited Liability Act was passed in the UK in 1855 and finished it in 1867. Prior to the 1855 Act, there had probably not been more than about 1,200 joint-stock companies formed since 1720.[9] A decade later, the number had risen exponentially. Between 1866 and 1874 there were on average around 800 new companies established by a process of incorporation in Britain *every year*.[10] As journalist Oliver Bullough has pointed out, in 1860, at least half of stock market trading in London was in government bonds; by 1914, 95% of trading was in corporate shares.[11] Indeed, around two thirds of British national wealth was invested in shares by the end of the nineteenth century.[12] Those shareholdings channelled the new wealth of industrialisation and colonisation accumulated by the booming merchant class, the new captains of industry and the growing middle class.

Historical analysis of climate change very often focuses on the period of European industrialisation as a departure point for understanding what is happening today. It is true that this is when we begin to see the beginning of an economy that is based on emitting carbon into the atmosphere. But one of the reasons that this book foregrounds the case of Stora Kopparberg, the world's first documented corporation, is to point to a much more stretched history. The most significant period of emissions is stretched into the future, in the centuries beyond the industrial revolution. As journalist David Wallace-Wells points out, more than half of the CO_2 in the air was produced in the past 3 decades.[13] This is the period that social scientists and economists lazily named an era of "globalisation". It is also a period in which the economic grip of the Global North over the Global South has tightened. And this is why a longer understanding of history is important, one that integrates the history of colonialism with the history of capitalism.

Although the corporation only began to dominate the domestic economy in the nineteenth century, it was at least 2 centuries prior to this – at the advent of European colonialism – that the corporation began its journey as the primary vehicle for enabling capital to expand its reach across the globe. The so-called "first globalisation" period is identified by economists as the global movement of trade and financial investment that began at some point in the nineteenth century (a major spike in international trade is normally said to have begun in 1870) before a decline in 1914 precipitated by World War I.[14] By the end of this period, the corporation was established as the central institution through which capital was invested. In the years following World War I the corporation's influence grew: by the end of the 1930s, there were more than 1,000,000 registered corporations in the US.[15] Whilst the rest of the twentieth century may have been a particularly intense period of financial globalisation, as this chapter will show, European states had used colonial corporations to begin the process almost 3 centuries earlier.[16]

A rudimentary grasp of this historical development shows clearly that are some basic features of the colonial-capitalist system that tell us it is palpably not sustainable; that colonial capitalism is an intrinsically *ecocidal* system. In his series of notebooks written at the end of the 1850s, *Fundamentals of Political Economy Criticism* (more commonly known as *Grundrisse*), Karl Marx describes the inherent tendency in capitalism to push back any barriers or limits that stand in its way. The driving force of capital is a continual process of expansion into new places where it can extract natural resources and make things, and into new markets.

> Capital by its nature drives beyond every spatial barrier. Thus, the creation of the physical conditions of exchange – of the means of communication and transport – the annihilation of space by time – becomes an extraordinary necessity for it.[17]

Marx argued that the capitalist economic system had an in-built tendency: that capital would always seek to break through any geographical barrier that stood in its way. His analysis reflected upon how transportation and communication in international commodity markets continually required the diminishing of space (or in Marx's terms "annihilation") between where something is produced and where it is sold or used. When we are able to eat string beans from a farm 6,000 miles away in Kenya, just two days after they were picked, this is the annihilation of space by time. When a stock market can enable shares in the corporation that exported the beans to be sold a fraction of a second after those shares had been bought, this is the annihilation of space by time. And when those shares are bought and sold from a computer terminal in New York 7,300 miles away from the farm in Kenya and 3,500 miles away from the company headquarters in London, this is the annihilation of space by time.[18]

The shrinking of time and space by capital is not merely an effect of the drive to reproduce itself. It is a *necessary* part of the process of reproducing capital. The continual process of reducing the time to buy and sell things and the incursion into new spaces where natural resources can be extracted, where new factories can be established, and where new markets can be created, is necessary precisely because capital *must* reproduce itself. It cannot stand still. This is a dynamic driving force of capitalism: capitalists invest their wealth in order to either maintain their position or to improve it. And if wealth, in the form of capital, is to reproduce itself, it must continue to make money from money. This is not a straightforward process in a world in which almost everyone with wealth is trying to increase their own share. As wealth increases, so the magnitude and energy of its growth increases; as does the wealth available to other capitalists. And so, capital seeks ever expanding opportunities to reproduce itself at a continually accelerating pace in continually shrinking spaces.

Put differently, this is a way of understanding the ecological consequences of growth economics. The view that capital's drive to expansion is unsustainable is quickly becoming a mainstream view. It is certainly not controversial anymore to assert that the economic growth paradigm is impossible to decouple from environmental destruction.[19]

In all of this, the important point that both Marx and more mainstream contemporary thinkers make is that capital is insatiable; it is ultimately incapable of ever being satisfied. It is this in-built impetus towards the reproduction of capital that means the boundaries of wealth production – the barriers to capital – are always pushed to their limit. As sociologist John Bellamy Foster has noted, the greater the energy of capital's expansion, "the greater are capital's ecological demands, and the level of environmental degradation".[20] The natural world is just a limit to be overcome in the same way as a spatial limit; everything and anything might be destroyed by the "juggernaut of capital".[21] In a very orthodox Marxist sense, the drive to destroy nature is an impulse that is based on the drive to expand production. It is in the drive to extract minerals from the earth, to rip up forests, to develop industrial scale agriculture, and to expand the capacity of factories to make things, that we see the insatiable appetite of capital for "devouring" nature.

Nature can only be devoured at this rate if there are consumer markets every bit as ravenous. The US economic sociologist James O'Connor has shown how the relentless expansion of capital, particularly in the twentieth century, has led to a kind of "hyper-capitalism" in which circles of consumption are ever-expanding.[22] In this sense, capitalism "tends to maximize the overall toxicity of production and to promote accelerated habitat destruction, creating problems of ecological sustainability".[23] In this process, both nature and workers are robbed of the conditions that enable them to live, as "polluted air and water" becomes the mode of existence for workers in industrial capitalism.[24]

Corporations are essential conduits for the global mobility of capital; they seek to move freely across borders, making global spaces smaller for investors, and speeding up the time needed to develop or extract resources, enabling them to locate production across the globe. It is this capacity of capital – the annihilation of space by time – which was perhaps the most important single dynamic in the development of European colonialism. And in the course of the colonial project, corporations could be relied on to overcome every natural barrier that stood in their way; corporations were mobilised by the colonial powers for the annihilation of nature and the annihilation of people on an unprecedented scale. Corporations have been, since the early seventeenth century, a central driving force in the struggle to overcome *nature's* limits.

If we are to fully grasp the ecocidal tendencies of the corporation, we need to understand that this dynamic of *annihilation* was the *modus operandi* of the colonial corporation. The annihilation of time and space in order to enable the annihilation of nature and people is *the* method by which corporations reproduce capital. It is to a deeper understanding of how this method was developed in the early colonial period that the chapter now turns.

Corporate racial exploitation

In 1721, English inventor James Puckle set up a joint-stock company to attract investment in a new weapon that used the first machine gun technology. The whole premise on which Puckle's gun was based was racist. He designed it to enable the operator to shoot two types of bullets for use in two types of wars. Round bullets could be shot at European Christians, and square bullets at Muslim Turks. The square bullets were designed to cause more devastating injuries. The barrel of the gun was engraved with the motto: "Defending King George, your country and lawes is defending yourselves and the protestant cause".[25] It was the perfect gun for a racist, colonial state.

Puckle had no trouble attracting investors to this project. Indeed, his company was one of thousands of schemes, inventions and adventures at the turn of the seventeenth and eighteenth centuries that sought to attract investment through a shareholder model. In the end, Puckle's invention was rejected for government and military use, not for lack of enthusiasm for a machine that sought to intensify the violence of its user's racism, but more simply because the mechanism did not work properly. The lack of any prospect of a contract to make the guns meant that the company collapsed. Every penny of investment in the company had been spent on the development of Puckle's gun. It was a typical event in an age of failed schemes. Although the market in joint-stock shares was not a particularly significant part of the economy in the late seventeenth/early eighteenth century, there was a proliferation of share ownership schemes in this period. As early as 1695, there were said to be more than 150 English companies whose shares were being dealt in the coffee shops around London's "Exchange Alley".[26] Many of those schemes turned out to be fraudulent, or unsuspecting investors at least were purchasing shares for ventures that had no serious chance of generating a capital return.

Perhaps the most famous of those failed schemes is the South Sea Company, formed in 1711 with the British government's promise of a monopoly on trade in South America. This story starts with the ongoing war with Spain. At the time, the Spanish controlled most of South America, including all of the main Atlantic ports. However, the end of the War of the Spanish Succession and subsequent Treaty of Utrecht of 1713 granted Britain a licence to supply the Spanish colonies with 4,800 slaves per year. The value of the South Sea Company's share price rose quickly with the promise that port concessions could be secured. In 1718 war broke out with Spain again and the company's assets in South America were seized. As soon as the company was refused access, the share price collapsed and the event, known as the "South Sea Bubble", precipitated the first stock market crash. The collapse of the South Sea Company led the British Parliament to take action against this form of speculative investment. A subsequent parliamentary inquiry found that a number of politicians, officials and company officers had profited unlawfully from the company and their assets were confiscated as a result. The 1720 Bubble Act banned the buying and selling of shares by anyone who was not involved in the management or direction of the company. The Act led to a number of companies being wound up or taken into ownership of the Crown. In the hundred or so years following the Bubble Act, the issue of charters was largely limited to large scale public works and building projects. Any partnerships tended to be unincorporated, and although these were numerous, in practice, Parliament regulated those associations and considered legal matters pertaining to them on a case by case basis. The Bubble Act was eventually repealed in 1825 and the practice of unhindered buying and selling of shares was once again legalised. The 1844 Joint Stock Companies Act allowed this model of investment without the need for a charter. Under the 1844 Act, companies could now simply establish a constitution and apply to the government body, the Registrar of Joint Stock Companies for incorporated status.

In standard historical accounts, the South Sea Bubble is described as the first stock market crash; in more critical histories, it is used as the archetypal example to indicate the fundamental instability of financial markets. Yet critical histories rarely highlight precisely what those "victims" of the South Sea Bubble sought to profit from. The main purpose of the South Sea Company was to expand British control of the slave trade from the Caribbean and North America into South America. Those "victims" were rubbing their hands at the prospect of a major expansion in the human slave trade. Indeed, the South Sea Company prospectus promised a monopoly on the supply of slaves to Spanish plantations for 30 years. The investors knew they were investing in a scheme to ship 145,000 slaves from Africa to South America. They would not have described themselves as such, but those investors were slave traders. The fact that history characterised the plight of those investors as victims and not slave traders is hugely significant. The partial history of the South Sea Company, and indeed, the more general failure of those histories to recognise the racist colonial utility of the joint-stock corporation and the savage logic that shaped its form has allowed historians to miss the point of the corporation.

The point of the corporation is to reduce both the financial exposure and the moral accountability of investors and enable them to look the other way. In the process of buying stock in a corporation, an important social relationship is established. Investors put money into a joint fund for one reason: because they expect a good return on this investment. In the process, they do not need to have anything do with the way their money is spent. As shareholders, they have the right to turn up at an annual general meeting to vote on some strategic issues, such as the composition of the board of directors. But if they choose not to, they don't need to know anything about the affairs of the corporation. They do not need to think of themselves as slave traders, merely as anonymous investors.

Just as the corporation is the institution that assists capital to disregard the limits of geography, or labour supply, or resource scarcity, at the same time the corporation enables capitalists to disregard moral limits or indeed any limits on their profiteering that we might expect to be consistent with a basic sense of humanity. Capital pushes beyond both *moral* limits and limits of *humanity*. There is no less polemical way to put this: the corporation is the perfect mechanism for a brutally violent, racist colonial state. As the Marxist international lawyer Robert Knox points out, colonial racism was always "part and parcel of the logic of capital accumulation".[27] This is also the basic fact of the corporation. Corporate racial exploitation is buried deep in the foundations of the history that made capitalism. This basic fact must be understood in order to understand the corporation's parallel drive to overcome *nature's* limits.

The colonising machine

From the late 1500s onwards, the corporation became the preferred organisational model that was used by the European colonial powers to enclose land, organise slavery and monopolise trade. The colonial corporations were established to open new trade routes and to settle new lands for the English, and latterly, British, Crown. They included the Company of Merchant Adventurers to New Lands, chartered in 1553 to open up a new trade route to China and Indonesia. This company was a partnership of 240 investors, each of whom invested £25 in exchange for a share in the company. The East India Company, chartered in 1600, probably the most infamous of the colonial companies, was granted exclusive rights to trade and to establish trading posts in the Indian sub-continent and South East Asia. As such, the East India Company played a crucial role in establishing the forms of commodity extraction and land-grab upon which the British Empire was founded. In order to build the capacity for the expansion of commerce and trade, most of the colonial corporations were given a monopoly on their trade. The London Company and the Plymouth Company were established to open up monopoly trading routes to the Americas. The State of Virginia was founded by the Virginia Company in 1607 and the State of Massachusetts by the Massachusetts Bay Company in 1628.[28] Those companies were granted charters by the Crown that gave them "the right to transport settlers and their supplies into the colonies, with the power to defend them".[29] Indeed, the right to bear arms enshrined in the second amendment of the US constitution uses a strikingly similar formulation to the constitution of the Massachusetts Bay Company.[30] It is in this model of the colonial corporation that the state delegated its own monopoly over the right to use legalised violence.

Many of the British and other European colonial corporations operated on a joint-stock basis. The various Dutch colonial trading enterprises amalgamated under one joint-stock corporation, the United East Indies Company, in 1612. In the early years of the English East India Company, wealthy merchants and the English ruling class owned the company's shares, and they were owned on a temporary basis. In 1657 it was established as a permanent joint-stock company. Advantages to investors were clear. Since the colonial companies were invariably given a monopoly over a trade route, or the governance over a resource-rich region, the returns were high.

The slavery market was developed and overseen by the African trading companies. Perhaps the most important of those, the Royal African Company, was established in 1662 by the English Crown and merchants from the City of London, originally to trade and mine gold on the west coast of Africa. By the 1680s, the company was trading 5,000 people as slaves every year. Although the company lost its monopoly twenty years after it was founded, because the right to trade slaves "was recognized as a fundamental and natural right of Englishmen",[31] by this time it had served its purpose as an "academy" for the large number of slave traders that followed it.[32]

The Royal African Company had established forts across West Africa, engaged in wars with trading rivals, particularly the Dutch, and between 1694 and 1700 was a major participant in the Komenda Wars in modern-day Ghana. The English (latterly, British) East India Company[33] was also to play a key role in the exercise of military and administrative control in India, acting as a proxy for English, latterly British, foreign policy. Throughout two and a half centuries, the East India Company was implicated in countless atrocities as part of an ongoing military suppression of local peoples until its rapid demise following the "Indian Rebellion" of 1857.[34] Its proxy colonial role on behalf of the British government gave it the necessary political cover to engage routinely in bribery and illegal trade.[35] Indeed, the company waged war against its French, Portuguese and Dutch counterparts to protect its access to raw materials and the factories and warehouses set up along the Indian coastline. As one history succinctly put it, the East India Company was the product of a contractual bargain with the state, despite existing "on constant life support, repeatedly having to justify its existence to the state".[36] It was their close alliance of mutual interest that enabled the colonial corporations to run their domains as the commissaries and direct representatives of the colonial state. Indeed, many of those companies had close connections to government ministers and the Royal family.[37]

The Indian Marxist economist Utsa Patnaik has carefully documented how a total of $45 trillion wealth was extracted from India during the colonial period.[38] This was a theft that has probably not been equalled in scale or audacity before or since. The East India Company played the key role in this grand theft. The company would pay artisans, farmers and merchants for raw materials and products and export them. The money they used to pay them was then taken back from local people as taxes. For investors, this was therefore the perfect no-risk business model.

Other colonial companies used stolen land as collateral to under-write a no-risk business model. Although the Virginia Company leaked money in its early days, the board simply parcelled up land and gave each investor 100 acres per share. Most of those shareholders planted tobacco, a key commodity in the North American slave trade. The Massachusetts Company upped its game by providing 200 acres of land for each share.[39]

The capture of new territories and the securing of trade routes was a competitive business that required a *national* mobilisation of capital. Those companies were established to enable the burden of economic risk in the colonies to be spread more broadly and to be absorbed by the state and by private wealthy individuals. This, in essence, is why the first limited liability companies were created: to enable private investors to shoulder the financial burden that alone the Crown could barely afford during this period of rapid global expansionism. The joint-stock corporation gave the state the financial capacity to colonise faster and further afield; the colonial corporation harnessed the veracity of capital's drive to reproduce itself.[40] In the capture of foreign territories, in the treatment of their rivals and of the native occupants of the lands they seized, the corporation could be ruthless and indifferent to the human consequences of the colonial project.

The consequences of corporate colonisation for human ecosystems was disastrous. Corporate colonisation was based upon the enclosure of traditionally owned and managed land. This meant exerting absolute control over forests and farmlands, rivers and lakes. The colonial corporation was crucial to this process of agricultural industrialisation in the Americas, in India and in Africa.[41] In a famous passage that became known as the "Lauderdale paradox",[42] Scottish politician James Maitland, 8th Early of Lauderdale wrote in 1804 that the Dutch East India Company was destroying crops at a time of plenty, and that the Virginia Company burned a proportion of their tobacco crop in order to maintain scarcity, and therefore a healthy price for their product. The apparent paradox that this presented to economists of the time was that the public interest (plentiful and cheap supply of crops) always suffers in the drive for private gain (the manipulation of scarcity and price).

In *Capital*, Marx had written extensively on a very different paradox. He witnessed a cycle that later generations of economists might have called "creative destruction". The rapid development of industrial agriculture was causing the exhaustion of soil. This led to a boomerang effect in which new nitrite-based nutrients were added, and the soil exhausted further. Larger quantities of nutrients would then need to be added to the soil, thus continuing a self-destructive cycle. This was a paradox that affected the new industrial farmers of Britain and the US most acutely. The only way to deal with the problem of soil exhaustion, without reverting to traditional methods of agriculture, was to "mine" bird droppings (guano) from islands off the coast of Peru and latterly Chile and replenish the soil artificially with nitrites. Indentured Chinese workers in the guano islands absorbed the appalling human costs of this trade. John Bellamy Foster and his colleagues concluded that this was a typical example of "ecological imperialism" that brutally gave impetus to the "enormous net flow of ecological resources from South to North" and facilitated labour conditions that Marx called "worse than slavery".[43] Crucial to this story was that the extraction of guano from Peru's islands and coastline was organised by colonial trading companies. The trade to Britain was organised by Anthony Gibb and Son (now part of the transnational insurance firm Marsh and McLennan) and to the US by Grace Brothers and Company (now the US chemical firm W.R. Grace and Company). Those corporations provided the necessary capital investment and as part of the deal offset part of the Peruvian national debt. In doing so they were the motor force behind this bold attempt to overcome nature's limits.

The argument in this chapter is not that this cycle of never-ending "creative destruction" could not have happened without the corporation. The European states would most likely have committed the atrocities of colonisation without being aided and abetted by corporations. Yet, at the same time, it is undeniable that corporations were crucial to the speed and the force with which colonisation proceeded. From the period of early European colonialism onwards, close and mutually reinforcing relationships between corporations and nation states have been the key powerbrokers in capitalist states.

Indeed, there is a relatively hidden history of the twentieth century that reveals the collusion of major corporations with the most brutal of states. It is a story in which many of the largest household name corporations have collaborated and supported the most brutal and violent states and have participated in the most reviled acts of war and even genocide. It is a history that reveals how the limitless expansion of capital pushes corporations to make profits from the most notorious totalitarian regimes, even when they are the governments of "enemy" states.

The tyrannical corporation

In the previous chapter, we noted that ChevronTexaco have been implicated in the cultural genocide of two Amazon tribes that no longer exist, the Tetetes and the Sansahuari. This is by no means the only human atrocity that the company was linked to in the twentieth century. In 1935, Texaco signed a deal with the Spanish Republican government that would have made Texaco its major fuel supplier.[44] Texaco was so desperate to sell the oil into Spain, that a year later it changed sides, breaking the US embargo against the Spanish dictator Francisco Franco. Texaco offered Franco oil on credit and used its network of tankers to smuggle fuel directly from American ports to nationalist Spain. The Franco regime was the regime that "disappeared" more people in the second half of the twentieth century than any state other than Cambodia.[45] For his services to the Fascist state, Franco awarded Texaco chairman Torkild Rieber the title of Knight of the Grand Cross of the Order of Isabella the Catholic.[46]

The centrality of domestic corporations in the rapid rise to power of the Italian and German Fascists was excavated as early as 1936 by French scholar Daniel Guerin in his classic account *Fascism and Big Business*.[47] However, Mussolini and Hitler were sustained not only by their own loyal businesses, but also by the patronage of international capital.[48] The roll call of names, of just the main corporate players, is astounding. The banks Union Bank of Switzerland, Credit Suisse,[49] Barclays Bank,[50] and Chase Bank (now JPMorgan Chase[51]) were implicated in assisting the theft of Jewish property. General Motors,[52] ITT,[53] Standard Oil of New Jersey (now ExxonMobil)[54] and, perhaps most famously, IBM,[55] are alleged to have knowingly provided vehicles, weapons, fuel and surveillance technology, without which the Nazi regime may not have been able to commit the holocaust.

Throughout the second half of the twentieth century, the most brutal, racist regimes across the globe have been readily supported by corporations. The racist regimes of South Africa and Rhodesia were sustained by US and European capital.[56] In Latin America and in Asia, Western corporations have been routinely implicated in the "disappearance" of trade unionists and community leaders in the fruit industry,[57] the soft drinks industry,[58] in the oil industry[59] and in clothing.[60] It is household names like Chichita, Del Monte, Coca-Cola, Dorothy Perkins and Primark that are implicated either directly, or via a supply chain relationship, in such disappearances. In Guatemala, Argentina and Brazil between 1964 and 1986 corporations were involved in hundreds of documented disappearances and assassinations. Amongst those mentioned in Argentina were local firms Ledesma and Dálmine, as well as Mercedes, Ford and Fiat.[61]

Less than 30 years after ITT's collaboration with the Nazis, Chilean socialist President Salvador Allende addressed the General Assembly of the United Nations. He took with him a document written by ITT officers in Chile and New York which proved that the company had authored an 18-point plan to strangle Chile economically, to carry out diplomatic sabotage, and create panic among the population, which would cause social disorder and precipitate a coup. A year later, the coup and the subsequent terror killed and "disappeared" over 20,000 people.[62] But what did the executives at ITT care, for the corporation was well rewarded by the regime, recovering a total of $235 million lost revenue and assets from the military junta.[63]

Salvador Allende's Chile was part of an anti-colonial movement of states in the developing world that sought to change a world order dominated by Western governments and Western corporations (and by the Soviet bloc) sometimes called the "Non-aligned movement". Allende himself was involved in a series of initiatives in the 1960s and 1970s that sought to reset the balance of power from an anti-capitalist and left-socialist perspective. This movement can be traced back to the 1955 Bandung Conference in Indonesia, which brought together 29 Asian and African states. Most of them had very recently gained political independence and together they represented 54% of the world's population. The 1966 Solidarity Conference of the Peoples of Africa, Asia and Latin America, or the "Tricontinental" as it became known, brought together representatives in Havana, Cuba, drawn from national liberation struggles and independent governments in 82 countries. Meetings like Bandung and the Tricontinental gave impetus to initiatives that explicitly sought to unravel the development of "neo-colonialism".

Neo-colonialism

The core idea of neo-colonialism, perhaps most famously articulated in Kwame Nkrumah's (1965) book of the same name,[64] was that colonialism had not ended with the liberation of former colonies that became "independent" in the late twentieth century. Colonisation had been perpetuated though economic and cultural strategies that removed the need for direct political rule. From the neo-colonial perspective, transnational corporations were viewed as mechanisms for advancing the colonial power of the developed world in more easily hidden and plausibly deniable forms. In a key passage, Nkrumah notes:

> The British Empire has become the Commonwealth, but the proceeds from the exploitation of British imperialism are increasing. Profits of British tin companies have ranged as high as 400%. The latest dividends to British diamond shareholders are close to 350%. On one occasion Mr Nehru [the Prime Minister of India 1947–1964] made it clear that British profits from independent India had more than doubled ... [A] recent survey made plain the plunder of British monopolies. It listed 9 out of 20 of Britain's biggest monopolies as direct colonial exploiting companies: Shell, British Petroleum,

British American Tobacco, Imperial Tobacco, Burma Oil, Nchanga Copper, Rhokana Corporation, Rhodesian Mines and British South Africa, five of which are directly engaged in chiselling away Africa's natural resources ... Incredibly the list leaves out two of the world's greatest combines, those states within a state – Unilever and Imperial Chemical Industries – whose operations are based heavily in their overseas exploitations. The United Africa company leads for Unilever in Africa; about a third of I.C.I. and its subsidiaries operate overseas.[65]

Nkrumah, who was President of Ghana and an important figure in the movement of unaligned states, offended the US State Department so much with his book that it immediately cut $25m in aid to the country.

It also became clear from the 1960s onwards that the mere fact of having abundant natural resources would not necessarily lead to post-colonial emancipation. As the example of countless African and Asian states demonstrates, the structure of corporate capitalism ensures what has come to be known as a "resource curse".[66] The model and its effects are always the same. Big Oil (or Big Mining or Big Diamonds) arrive on the scene with the finance and the technical know-how to develop the "resource". From this point on, the economy is driven by corruption, power is concentrated in narrow elites, and most of the money leaves the country anyway. Indeed, much of it leaves through the back door via a combination of opaque corporate structures and shady offshore trusts.[67] The population is normally left poor and the land and water supplies poisoned. This might seem like a cynical summation of the resource curse, yet it is a pattern that is repeated time and time again.

Militarised conflicts in the Global South are almost all resource conflicts. Even when they look like "ethnic" or "religious" conflict, they are almost invariably conflicts over the control of resources. And the intervention of Global North countries in global conflict is normally for the same reason, albeit positioned in a language of "humanitarianism" or "self-defence". Even when Global North countries are involved in conflicts where access to resources is not immediately at stake, the geo-strategic aim always involves access to resources.[68] And today, as has been the case in the history of colonialism, it is the corporation that plays a key role in securing access to those resources. Although it was controversial to claim it at the time, we now know, due to the release of government documents, that major figures in the US and UK oil companies had been involved in the planning of the invasion and the securing of the oil fields in the 2003 Iraq War.[69] And we know that UK ministers intervened directly on behalf of the British oil company BP in the negotiations of the carve-up of Iraq's oil fields.[70] In almost every region where there is oil, there is also conflict. As we have seen already in this book, the Global North oil companies understand their role well, and across Latin America, Africa and Asia are implicated in a large number of oppressive regimes and low intensity militarised conflicts. Those resource wars are now poised to be fought over water and food, as well as minerals.[71]

A number of initiatives emerged in the UN in the 1970s that sought to deal with the problem of neo-colonialism generally, and the grip of transnational corporations on the resources of the developing world in particular. But they faced a rising tide of neoliberal political and economic practices pushed by the US and its allies, known as the Washington consensus.[72]

The neo-colonial model has characteristics that are common across industries and across geographical contexts. First, the corporation gains the political support of the host state. A host nation state permits natural resources or local labour to be exploited, or facilitates the opening up of local markets for products because of some perceived economic or political advantage. This advantage may be measured in the form of power and influence, the potential for increasing the GDP or earnings potential for a state, or in some cases it may simply be measured in favours and bribes. Corporate bribes are ubiquitous across a number of industries. Second, those advantages accrue disproportionately to elites rather than the local population, and often the process of resource exploitation and development is opposed by the people living in the locale. The process of neo-colonisation therefore commonly involves conflict between the host state and the local people. Third, the home states in which corporations are primarily based provide a number of political and economic incentives to both corporations and to the elites of host states. The former may involve the mobilisation of diplomatic support, and export subsidies and credit guarantees; the later may involve aid, lobbying and fine-print negotiations in trade deals and the promise of strategic military or geo-political alliances. As we have seen, the neo-colonial model has required the enforcement capacities of host military forces and paramilitaries in a number of contexts from Nigeria to Colombia.

Those three characteristics of neo-colonialism add up to a pattern of power-brokering that is remarkably consistent across all of the major industrial processes which pose the most acute problems for the eco-system. It is the same pattern of power-brokering that characterises the oil and gas industries across the world's oil producing regions and enables big agriculture and chemical companies to facilitate the uncontrolled global spread of toxic fertilisers and pesticides. The same pattern of power-brokering characterises all major inward investment initiatives in the Global South.

Local autonomy over agriculture in the Global South, previously granted as a concession under the direct rule of colonial corporations and occupier governments, is now eradicated completely by a combination of voracious corporate land grabs, predatory pricing and asymmetric trade deals that leave local farmers at the mercy of international capital.[73] Local farming traditions are eradicated, while wholly unsustainable models of farming become globalised.[74] The corporate control of global agriculture is argued by some food economists to be the most significant contributor to global warming.[75] Big Agri – the international agriculture industry – is responsible for driving processes that irreversibly poison lakes and rivers and exhaust the fertility of land, creating a cycle of chemical use to compensate for a lack of nutrients, which then kills more nutrients. The history of the Peruvian guano industry is repeating itself, except this time no nation state is able to exert control over the supply chain. It is the large corporations who have the most control over those markets, and yet they themselves are locked into this cycle of creative destruction. Neo-colonialism, like its antecedents contains the seeds of environmental disaster, devouring land and water and people, and leaving behind a devastated eco-system.

The construction of large industrial dams has a similar dynamic. Dams, like most major infrastructure projects, displace and destroy important habitats and evict communities. Arundhati Roy observed in 2001 that "big dams in India have displaced not hundreds, not thousands, but millions – more than 30 million people in the last fifty years. Almost half of them are Dalit and Adivasi, the poorest of the poor".[76] Millions more have been displaced since.

Perhaps the most aggressive products marketed in the neo-colonial period are "soft" drinks. The pattern of the marketing strategy traditionally (since the 1960s at least) has followed a similar path: target marketing strategies at the young and especially the more affluent sections of the population and then work out to other groups from there, until the product is completely assimilated into the culture. In recent years, companies like Coca-Cola are not just content with establishing their standard brands (Coke, Sprite, Fanta etc), but follow complex diversified strategies that introduce a more varied range of products into the market. Coca-Cola is currently embarking on a $5 billion investment strategy in India – which it aims to make its third biggest global market after the US and Mexico – to introduce new brands and new tastes, including the "Indian" fruit juice-based drink "Minute Maid Mosambi".[77] All of this sounds very innocent (no pun intended) until we take account of the social and environmental impact of Coca-Cola in India. Its plants in India and Mexico, in particular, have been widely condemned for their intense use of local water supplies, which depletes groundwater to perilously low levels and releases polluting chemicals into the water system.[78] In many plants, they give the by-product of toxic sludge to local farmers as "fertiliser". This creates a dangerous chemical feedback loop. One NGO, the Centre for Science and Environment, tested carbonated drinks made by Coca-Cola and PepsiCo at 25 of their bottling plants and reported a "cocktail of between three to five different pesticides in all samples".[79] The Coca-Cola plant in Uttar Pradesh was closed down after regulators found that high levels of cadmium, lead and chromium and the "excessive" depletion of groundwater by the plant had led to water shortages and exacerbated droughts.[80]

In India – as is the case in much of the Global South – many of the most immediate and direct threats to the environment stem directly from consumer markets. The scandal of "sachet packaging" is the paradigm example.[81] Companies such as Unilever have begun to issue small sachets of products normally available in larger packs, such as soap powder or shampoo, for sale to people who can't afford the normal sized packets of those products. Because the packaging is generally plastic, and based on a high volume of smaller packs, the result is that drains are blocked and water supplies polluted more easily and intensively with discarded packaging, and waste is multiplied.[82] Of course, it is the communities that corporations target in aggressive marketing strategies, the communities that need smaller (i.e. cheaper) pack sizes, who suffer the most.

The end point of the relentless drive for profits is the creation of new consumer markets that at the same time exploit poverty and make the conditions for the poor even worse. Those are the consumer markets that we have begun to realise are deadly for both people and for the planet. This model of neo-colonialism not only threatens the sustainability of the industry itself, but now threatens the future of the planet.

The ecocidal corporate chain

In contrast with the classical colonial model, transnational corporations have morphed into forms that allow them to push beyond any moral or legal limits on what they do. The modern forms adopted by corporations operating in neo-colonial contexts typically use complex ownership chains and/or sit at the head of supply chains in which a number of parties are responsible for organising the production of commodities and of manufactured goods. Those complex ownership and supply chains maximise the ability of transnational corporations to distance themselves from responsibility for their environmental impacts, since often the most devastating impacts of corporate activity are not organised directly by corporations, but are organised by subsidiaries, or by other parties in the supply chain.

This is the issue in the garment industry, when sportswear companies like Nike or Adidas, or high street stores like H&M and Primark use complex supply chains to ensure their goods are produced in the most cost-effective way. The companies that they contract to do carry out this work produce goods to highly detailed specifications. Included in those specifications are average times taken to produce garments at each stage of the process, and costs that are apportioned for each part of the process, worked out to fractions of seconds and dollars. In other words, although the supply chain may be micro-managed at a level one would normally expect only to find inside the organisational structure, the supply chain ensures that they relate to each other as separate contracting parties (though in practice they are obviously part of the same enterprise). The point is that those companies can and do plausibly deny any knowledge of what is happening further down the "supply chain", and formally are not responsible for employees' pay and conditions. Supply chains and chains of ownership effectively insulate primary owners and buyers from liability for violations of rights at the labour-intensive end of the supply chain. The same goes for their responsibilities to the eco-system.

The destruction of forests accounts for 10–15% in the rise in global greenhouse gas emissions.[83] And deforestation occurs in order to meet Western corporations' demand for raw materials. Four types of products are responsible for 70% of tropical forest loss: beef and cattle, timber, palm oil and soy (mainly used for animal feed).[84] Some of the companies most implicated, like MacDonalds (one of the largest buyers of beef and chicken feed produced in deforested land) have been constantly in the spotlight. Yet only 30% of the companies that have an impact on tropical forests know exactly where their supply chain begins.[85] Just like the Peruvian Rubber Company corporate executives and investors who, as we saw in the previous chapter, had no incentive to know anything about the devastation that their company was causing, the same goes for today's corporate elite. They don't need to know.

In Peru today, like any other Global South economy, we can find numerous examples of an ecocidal corporate chain. Let us briefly examine gold mining. The gold mining industry in Peru is in the midst of a crisis that links an epidemic of worker deaths to a biodiversity catastrophe. A huge network of illegal gold mines has been established in Madre de Dios in South East Peru. This network of mines is responsible for the destruction of around 170,000 acres of primary rainforest in the Peruvian Amazon between 2013 and 2018.[86] In addition, the use of mercury in the production process pollutes lakes and rivers, affecting the fish, a major source of the diet of local people. One study by Peru's Ministry of Health found that 78% of the local Nahua community had dangerously high levels of mercury in their blood.[87]

This network of small-scale (or "artisanal") mining needs no major investment or heavy equipment and has relied on a steady stream of poor workers from the Andean highlands to sustain it. It is estimated that there are tens of thousands of child labourers in Peruvian artisanal gold mines, and there are widespread reports of forced labour conditions.[88] Appalling working conditions mean the risks of death and injury are high. Major risks include poor ventilation, long working hours, malaria, and mercury poisoning. Research shows that exposures to silica – the cancer-causing dust – are probably over 200 times greater in artisanal mines than in large mines.[89] Victims of silica suffer a very long and very painful death. This is not just an epidemic-waiting-to-happen in Peru. There are at least

15 million "artisanal" miners working worldwide, a figure that is many times more than those employed in formal sector mines. Those workers tend to be working without any dust control measures, are rarely protected by a trade union, and very often have no legal protection whatsoever.[90]

The story of Peru's illegal gold mining, where slave labour-like conditions are the norm, is not, as first appears, a story of mercenary local gangsters and people smugglers. This is part of the story. But it is much more obviously a story of complex *corporate* structures. As in all global supply chains, there are large corporations – normally based in the Global North – at the top end of the chain. Those corporations take the highest cut. Insight Crime, a group of investigative journalists dedicated to uncovering organised crime in Latin American allege that those corporations either profiting from or financing the mines include: Metalor Technologies and MKS Finance from Switzerland; Northern Texas Refinery Metals and Republic Metals Corporation from the US; Italpreziosi from Italy and the Kaloti group based in Dubai.[91]

Those companies at the top of the supply chain universally rely on a complex corporate structure that spans the length of the chain. Further investigations by Insight Crime have shown that "shell" mining companies[92] are incorporated in Peru to give financiers the plausible excuse that they are using legitimate companies. The revenue is channeled through those shell companies although they are not doing any actual mining;

the mining is done by illegal companies that are unincorporated. This is a clear example of how the corporate structure is perfectly designed to mask accountability and to create distance between the real beneficiaries of the supply chain and the point of production.

Precisely the same principle is applied when complex corporate chains are organised through secrecy jurisdictions, otherwise known as tax havens. It is estimated that 101 companies quoted on the London Stock Exchange control over $1 trillion worth of minerals extracted from Africa in five commodities (oil, gold, diamonds, coal and platinum).[93] In total, $46 billion a year leaves African countries as multinational company profits,[94] with approximately 60% of the value of those funds as tax avoidance, funnelled through offshore companies.[95] A further $35 billion a year leaves African countries in illicit financial flows.[96] Tax havens enable the extraction of both illicit and legitimate wealth in this form to be hidden through a web of complex corporate structures. It normally works like this: a "shell" company is established somewhere like the Seychelles or the Cayman Islands, and then a complex web of other parent and subsidiary "shell" companies are established in a number of secrecy jurisdictions to create a long ownership chain. The result is that the origins of the extracted wealth and the beneficiaries at the end-point of the chain cannot be connected. No matter how environmentally destructive those investments, the source of the profit remains hidden from plain sight.

Investors are able to maximise wealth extraction precisely because the corporations they invest in are able to maintain a position at the head of the corporate ownership structure, or at the head of the supply chain. Those subsidiary chains and supply chains are the mode that transnational corporations based in Global North countries use to extract resources, deplete nature and risk environmental catastrophe. And typically, this destruction takes place in the Global South, or, when it comes to the change in weather systems, its effects are felt most in the Global South. At the same time, those complex corporate structures enable the steady growth of industrial development and investor return regardless of the human and environmental cost.

Conclusion: the perfect vehicle for devouring nature

There is a very clear nexus of capitalist development that links colonialism, genocide and ecocide.[97] The vital life force at the heart of this nexus is the corporation. Naomi Klein talks of the "braided historical threads of colonialism, coal and capitalism".[98] In this braided history, the corporation is the loom.

As this chapter has argued, the motor force of the corporation is driven by the necessity for capital to reproduce itself. And as part of this ongoing reproduction of capital, corporations are involved in a continual struggle to overcome *nature's* limits. As we have seen, the capitalist corporation was absolutely central to the long project of European colonisation. Indeed, it was through the European colonial project that the corporation became *the* primary vehicle used by investors and by colonising governments to devour nature and human labour. The extraction of natural resources, particularly from colonised lands, was done on a scale and at a rate that would not have been possible without the colonial corporation.

The architecture of the corporation made it ideal for colonial adventure; in its current form it is perfectly designed for a neo-colonial world. As it has adapted complex subsidiary and supply-chain structures, the corporation has vastly expanded its capacity to overcome the limits on the global mobility of capital and limits on resource scarcity. This adaptation of the modern corporation has expanded its capacity to devour nature, as if there were no limits to the exploitation of nature itself. At the same time, investors are even more empowered to disregard any moral limits placed upon them or indeed disregard basic values of humanity.

3

Regulation at the end-point of the world

When Stora Enso opened the Montes del Plata mega-mill in 2014, the Uruguayan President José Mujica was at the opening ceremony, along with most of his cabinet and a host of local government officials. This was, after all, the largest single industrial investment in the country's history, projected to be worth 2% of GDP. The Uruguay government's willingness to provide economic support to Montes del Plata was underlined by the plant's designation as a "free-trade zone".[1] In other words, this designation gave Stora, and its partner in the venture, Arauco, "special" tax exemptions. Free-trade zones typically grant other incentives, and may include exemptions from export restrictions, labour law and environmental regulations. In other words, free-trade zones are like a carrot dangled in front of foreign capital: if you invest, we can get rid of the nuisance of regulation.

We don't know whether Stora was offered any incentives other than tax breaks for Montes del Plata. Yet certainly the Uruguay government was keen to downplay the major environmental problems associated with the wood pulp industry. At the opening of the plant President Mujica announced: "humanity recovers the disasters it creates, that is why it reveres those who rebuild, think, dream and make long-term sacrifices for the future".[2] He didn't specify exactly what those sacrifices were, or indeed exactly what this meant for the future. Given what we know about the wholesale destruction of local eco-systems and local ways of life, it is safe that local farmers and indigenous peoples will be the ones making the sacrifices. And those sacrifices are certainly not being made for their, or for the planet's future.

The relationship between Stora and its host government in Uruguay is typical of relationships between transnational corporations and governments in the Global South. In virtually all of the examples mentioned so far in this book, corporations have been encouraged and incentivised, by both the governments in the countries they are based in and by their host governments, to deplete natural resources, destroy habitats and exploit local people. Stora Enso's relationship with its host government is also very significant; it is part owned by both the Finnish and Swedish governments. Stora's relationships with its home and host governments capture a crucial dynamic in ecocide that we have not fully explored yet: the role of government regulation.

In the previous chapter, we saw how colonial European states used colonial corporations to do their dirty work: to seize land, to settle colonising forces, to plunder resources, to impose regimes of non-wage and wage slavery, to establish labour camps, and so on. Such corporations were seen as the most expedient means of colonising Africa because they could administer trade, run local affairs, and conduct military operations without over-exposing the state either financially or politically. History has shown that those companies had little moral compunction and embarked upon brutal campaigns of terror wherever they met local resistance to the imposition of regimes.

We have forgotten this history too easily. In contemporary capitalism we tend to think about the role of governments in precisely the opposite terms: to protect people from the insecurities embedded in markets, and to protect us from the harmful things that corporations do. We are not entirely wrong to think in this way. As this chapter will show, there are serious consequences when governments don't intervene to protect us. To put it bluntly, when government regulation fails, people die.[3] It is clear that without the intervention of the governments in South America to protect large parts of the rainforest, the state of nature in that region would be much worse.

Yet the dominant mode of development, as we saw in the previous chapter and in the Stora Enzo example is that natural resources and land must be used for productive and profit making purposes. The way this is organised in global capitalism is through nation states providing the necessary legal and infrastructural capacities for corporations to produce and make profits. Governments do this, while at the same time offering (limited) protections to their citizens and to the environment. The point that is very often missed by commentators and scholars of regulation is that the protective role of the state cannot be understood in isolation from the deep relationship between governments and corporations. The process of regulation has a dual function: it both enables and controls environmental damage.

Licensed to kill

One group of Marxist economists and social scientists known as the "regulation school" argue that this is precisely the point of regulation. It is not merely to control harms, or to ensure that people or the environment are protected. Scholars like the economist Michael Aglietta argue that the primary purpose of regulation in capitalist societies is to govern and normalise the way that society is hierarchically ordered.[4] The process of regulation – the things that governments do to control markets and to control corporations is not just about the task of trying to *control* damage to the environment. The process of regulation also gives corporations permission to pollute within particular limits. Indeed, it is the conditions of such licences that form an important part of any regulator's work. As well as being responsible for *controlling* pollution and ensuring air and water quality is protected, the UK Environment Agency also issues 14,000 pollution licences every year. The holders of those licences are permitted to produce waste, or to discharge substances into the air or into waterways.[5]

In liberal democracies like the UK, even the most deadly forms of pollutant are produced under the conditions of a licence granted by a regulatory authority. For example, the Innospec plant, in Ellesmere Port in the North West England, is said to be the last factory in the world producing lead additives for petrol. The facility is licenced for this purpose, and exports the chemical to Algeria, despite the World Health Organization defining lead as a public health catastrophe.[6] The same chemical plant was, in the early 2000s, releasing some of the highest levels of carcinogenic chemicals in the UK. Just two chemical facilities run by Associated Octel (the previous name of Innospec) and Ineos, were permitted to emit 4 tonnes of dioxins into the British air annually.[7] Those factories alone accounted for the emission of 40% of the UK's dioxins into the air. And they were licenced by the British government to do so.

This is the paradox that lies at the heart of the regulatory process. Corporations are licenced to kill, albeit it within government defined limits. And those limits are not determined from a standpoint of public safety, or indeed of protecting the planet; they are determined by an economic standard. This is another principle that is increasingly being codified in regulatory systems.

Processes of regulation are therefore only ever partially concerned with efforts to "control" corporations. States play a much more expansive "regulatory" role that enables corporations to thrive. Indeed, as we saw in chapter 1, the state is the lifeblood of the corporation, from the point that it establishes the rules of incorporation. States establish all of the complex rules that allow markets to exist (laws of contract and property, the rules that government labour markets and commodity markets, and so on). States establish transport and communication infrastructures, organise diplomatic relationships with other states to enhance opportunities for import, export and investment, and set the rules for taxation and liability that, as we have seen, differ substantially from the rules that apply to individuals. Reregulation is often mistaken for deregulation. As corporate criminologist Steve Tombs notes, neoliberal policy making involves a huge amount of time and energy – a great deal of "intervention" – to strip away the regulation that protects us.[8] We cannot simplistically describe all of the energy that governments have spent in the neoliberal period to assist business as "de-regulation". Rather, it is re-regulation. There is no "roll-back" of the state at work here; the state is merely involved in a different type of regulation.

In 2015, the UK government introduced a new rule that all regulatory agencies had to comply with. This new rule was the so-called "growth duty", which was introduced into law in the Deregulation Act 2015. The growth duty requires all UK regulators to "have regard to the desirability of promoting economic growth".⁹ What this means is that front line inspectors at the Environment Agency and every other regulatory agency (including the Health and Safety Executive, the Financial Conduct Authority and the Serious Fraud Office) have to consider the impact of their decisions on the economic health of a business before they enforce the law. UK government rules now require regulators to formally report how their enforcement of the law might have impeded business. The problem here is that regulators have a dual function, and those functions have opposite aims: on one hand, the promotion of the growth of an industry, and on the other hand, the control of its harmful and criminal activities. It is this contradiction that makes some people pessimistic about our reliance on states to protect us.

In Colombia, strange things have been happening since a peace deal and ceasefire between left wing guerrilla group Revolutionary Armed Forces of Colombia (FARC) and the government was agreed in 2016. Because of the conflict, large parts of the forest in areas that were previously FARC territory had been protected from development. Quite simply, FARC protected its territory and it was too dangerous for developers to encroach on land that it controlled. Since the ceasefire, it is reported that there has been significant industrial development of parts of the wilderness that are crucial for sustaining bio-diversity. One analysis of the immediate impact of logging, gold-mining and cattle-grazing found that deforestation increased by

44% in 2016.[10] It is not an *absence* of the Colombian state that led to this, although in reality FARC was the *de facto* state authority prior to 2016. It is the post-2016 restoration of the Colombian state as the political authority that is encouraging deforestation for commercial purposes.

Ecocidal practices occur not just as a result of a breakdown in the regulatory function of states; they occur as part and parcel of a process of state power-mongering, and, in the main those practices are tolerated and encouraged by states. In other words, very often the environment is threatened not merely by the absence of the state, but rather by its presence. In Colombia, there is a long record of the state imposing a violent rule of law in collaboration with paramilitaries to enable the theft and exploitation of the land and the forced eviction of people who live there.[11] Put simply, state regulation in Colombia has facilitated the corporate ecocide. In different contexts, organised around different institutional axes, this is pretty much a universal principle of capitalism.

Witness the burning of the Amazon in August 2019, when it became apparent that the Jair Bolsonaro government in Brazil was particularly keen not to "intervene" to protect the forests from "slash and burn" rainforest clearance by commercial developers. Indeed, under Bolsonaro, the Brazilian government has cut the Brazilian environmental protection agency IBAMA budget by 95%,[12] and left fire services unable to cope with those slash and burn tactics. However, environmental destruction on this level is not possible without the state actively permitting it, either informally or secretly. As Bolsonaro frenetically briefed against the G8 governments threatening trade sanctions, an internal Brazilian government PowerPoint presentation was leaked to *democraciaAbierta*. The presentation revealed the Bolsonaro government's intention to use hate speech to isolate minorities in the Amazon, asserting that "a strong government presence in the Amazon region is important to prevent any conservation projects from taking root".[13]

Apparently, a great deal of intervention was being done to make sure that the Amazonian rainforest was not protected![14] Therefore, what counts is not the presence or absence of the government, but the *type* of presence.

Capitalism eats itself

Ultimately, the primary purpose of all forms of regulation in capitalist states is to ensure that capitalism thrives. In order to do so, the primary aim of regulation – understood in its totality – is to ensure a stable and uninterrupted system of production, distribution and consumption. Regulation therefore aims to protect the basic hierarchy and reproduce the social order. Of course, occasionally, some powerful individuals and institutions may be punished or banned from doing particular things at particular times, but even when states intervene to protect the environment, those interventions are not allowed to seriously disrupt regimes of profit accumulation.

And a very important aspect of this aim is, quite simply, to enable capital to reproduce itself, not least to stop it destroying the source of its own profits. This was Marx's central point in his analysis of the introduction of the nineteenth-century Factory Acts, the laws that imposed limits on the working hours of factory operatives. The factory-owning class, Marx wrote, was threatening to undo its own sustainability because of its "were-wolf hunger for surplus labour". By working their employees into an early grave, the factory masters were quite literally exhausting their own supply of labour, thus precipitating the "slow sacrifice of humanity".[15] In the English town of Stoke, he observed, most of those employed making ceramics in "the potteries" were being killed by pulmonary diseases caused by their work. The mortality rate was so high that each generation of potters was noticeably diminished in both numbers and productive capacity, when compared to the last. In the manufacture of everything, from wallpaper to hats, mortality rates were leading to shortages of labour. In matchmaking, mostly done by children, new diseases like lockjaw were produced by exposure to the phosphorous pits, making the average child's life expectancy not much over 18. Regulation was not just needed to stop people being worked to death for humanitarian reasons, or even because a more militant workforce demanded it. It was also necessary to stop the "limitless draining of labour power" by the factory masters who had "torn up by the roots the living force of the nation".[16]

There is a "double movement"[17] that arises in struggles for better regulatory standards. The first movement can be understood as a struggle for regulation from below – by communities and those most affected by environmental damage. When we demand and campaign for "more" regulation we do it because we know this can have real, material effects, which mitigate the human and environmental costs of capitalism. Whether we campaign as trade unionists demanding meaningful action on climate change, or as communities demanding tighter limits on emissions from industrial sites in our neighbourhoods, we know that that regulatory standards are necessary. Yet the paradox is found in the second movement: regulation also makes capitalism more durable. The second movement tends to come from within the state, or from powerful groups representing particular sectors of business. The outcome of the more carefully regulated system in the British factories was that workers continued to be injured and killed (albeit it at a lower, more sustainable rate), but that the system survived and indeed became more durable. In other words, regulation is imposed from above in order to stop capitalism eating itself.

Financing the ecocide

There is persuasive reason to believe that this double movement is unlikely to succeed as a stabilising force in the current stage of capitalism. In a typical factory system in the textile industry today, for example, or in any "offshored" system of manufacturing, the principle contractor at the top of the supply chain has no control or vested interest in sustaining the productivity of a particular group of workers. If workers are too ill or too tired to work, it simply engages another contractor in the supply chain, which could be in another region or another country. As the need for a stable and healthy workforce in this model of production is lessened, cycles of investment get shorter. And as the economy becomes more financialised – more focussed on financial rationales and financial motives – the demand for a quick return on investment intensifies. This is partly a result of the same process described in the previous chapter: as capitalism develops, increased competition tends to mean that in total the rate of return on capital decreases.

As the double movement of regulation is undermined by financialised models of development, capitalist industrial processes become more and more difficult to regulate.

As we saw in the previous chapter, corporate ecocide began with colonial corporation. And the colonial corporation was created to be nothing more or less than an investment structure. Indeed, as we saw in chapter 1, the raison d'être of the corporation is to provide an investment structure for capital. It is through the corporation that all of our most damaging threats to the eco-system are organised. And the continual expansion of those corporations and their associated operations are fueled by a financial sector of extraordinary complexity. The financing of almost every industrial process mentioned in this book has to be planned and put in place before a well is drilled, a new chemical is researched, or a new form of packaging is developed. Yet we have no regulatory structure that places limits on what can be financed and who can finance it.

Take, for example, the impact of financial models of development on the global agriculture and fishing business. Historically the World Bank has played a crucial role in encouraging and financing a relatively uncontrolled land grab for agriculture and fisheries.[18] The ownership of the farms is diversified across financial investors, and local farmers have little or no power to change the process. If food stocks are hit by disease, or overproduction causes sustainability problems, buyers simply buy elsewhere.[19] The regulation of the impact of investment on the environment is simply not part of this financial modelling. For example, it is estimated that 40% of the world's mangrove loss is attributed to shrimp farming alone.[20] Shrimp farming, like the rest of the global fish farming industry is based on a highly complex supply chain that is also highly financialised. That is, most fish farming is driven by short-term investments that are facilitated by global financial institutions.

Similarly, the price of commodities is regulated in ways that are more, rather than less, likely to drive climate change and create new eco-crises. High impact industrial processes are very often driven by sudden shifts in commodity markets. The exponential growth of the Peruvian artisanal mines discussed in the previous chapter, for example, resulted directly from a steep rise in the price of gold. Given that many of those mines were opened up in remote places and perhaps would be relatively difficult to prevent even if the state wanted to, high prices were the key drivers in this industry. Similarly, a sustained high oil price is what guarantees the perpetual profitability of fossil fuels. And we can see exactly the same process occurring in all industrial processes as commodities become scarcer.

The problem we have is that the regulatory mechanisms controlling financial investment flows, or the mechanisms that set the prices of things, don't even remotely take account of climate change or ecocide. This is partly a function of the problem of externalities set out in chapter 1. But it is also very simply a function of how governments decide what should be regulated as an environmental threat. If anything, global warming pushes the price of commodities like gold *up*. The same principle applies to carbon fuels. If climate change has any impact on the price of oil, it is to force it up. It is a combination of decisions made by the oil producing states, and geo-political circumstances like war or the threat of war, that set the price of oil.[21] And it is those geo-political factors that increase or decrease the chances of financial investments in fossil fuels, or any other production process that is threatening the future of the planet.

The political economy of speed

It is very common for industrial disasters to be linked to sharp changes in economic conditions. For example, the complex conditions that caused a massive explosion on an oil platform in the British North Sea in 1988 can be traced back to a sharp change in the price of oil. This explosion, on the Piper Alpha platform, killed 167 workers. It was the worst industrial disaster the UK had seen in a century. The collapse of the OPEC cartel quota three years before the Piper Alpha disaster saw the average price for a barrel of oil plummet from more than $30 in November 1985 to around $10 in April 1986. The implosion of the oil market had a dramatic effect on the industry. In order to defend profit levels, oil companies slashed their operational budgets by 30–40%.[22] Wage levels fell dramatically and 1986 saw up to 22,000 jobs lost in the industry.[23] The oil companies' response to the collapse in the oil price had far reaching implications for workplace safety in the industry, and budgets allocated to the regular maintenance of plant equipment were slashed. It is not difficult to see how the collapse of the market price can affect the balance of power between shareholders, managers and workers. When the oil price is low, the demand to make more profits for less investment intensifies.

This is not to say that environmental outcomes are determined by financial mechanisms alone. This is certainly not the case. Industrial processes that damage the environment are always the result of a complexity of processes that are both *economic* and *political*.

The roots of the Piper Alpha disaster in an aggressive, cost-cutting, management following the oil price crash is only one part of the story. Another important factor is how the corporate managements in charge of oil platforms like Piper Alpha were permitted to neglect safety in this way. Six years before the disaster, Irish socio-legal researcher Kit Carson wrote a remarkable book that more or less predicted the Piper Alpha disaster.[24] The production of oil in the North Sea, Carson wrote, had been allowed to push beyond its physical limits. Carson carefully documented the way that the UK oil industry had developed out of a balance of social forces that he described as the "political economy of speed". By using the term political economy, Carson was deliberately suggesting that both politics and economy combine powerfully to shape the priorities of corporate managements.

His book, *The Other Price of Britain's Oil*, argued that the political context had shaped the degree to which the oil companies were able to take risks. The UK government, in its desperation to get the oil out from under the sea, had deliberately ensured lax regulatory conditions and provided a number of commercial incentives and tax breaks to the oil companies. Another consequence of this political economy was a very clear decision not to control production at the start of the cycle, and therefore not to impose "depletion controls" that would limit the amount of oil produced over time.[25]

Carson had noted that British oil workers were paying the ultimate price for the political decision not to control the rate of production. Although the chance of being killed on an oil rig or platform was many times that of an equivalent onshore worker (eleven times the fatality rate in the construction industry and nearly nine times the rate in mining), the UK government effectively exempted offshore platforms from legal protections and turned a blind eye to union busting in order to maximise oil production. This political economy of speed created unbearable tensions which pushed the production process beyond its safe limits.

Almost precisely the same political and organisational conditions described above were repeated when BP's Deepwater Horizon exploded in the Gulf of Mexico. Similar characteristics (lax regulation, market instability, aggressive management cost-cutting) are present in countless industrial disasters;[26] an eerily similar combination of factors was present at the Bhopal chemical disaster in India, for example.[27] The political economy of speed is a concept that can be usefully expanded to explain the regulatory problem that we identified earlier in this chapter: very often workers, communities and their environments are threatened, not by the absence of the state, but rather by its presence.

Of course, profit-making ventures are always framed

by a political economy of speed. When forests are cleared at a pace too fast to be renewed, in order to meet a demand for mining or crop farming or cattle grazing, this is the political economy of speed at work. When industrial processes are developed to ensure that we can have mange tout on our plate within 48 hours of being picked, this is the political economy of speed at work. And when chemicals that end up in the atmosphere are produced because the alternatives take too long to develop, this is also the political economy of speed at work.

The political economy of speed is a concept that describes how political strategies interact with economic conditions in a way that shape the speed and intensity of production regimes. It describes how these strategies can alter the pace of production, the speed and scale of resource depletion, the chances of pollution occurring or being controlled, and so on. The important thing to grasp about this way of understanding industrial processes is that governments are never powerless. They always influence both economic and industrial outcomes. Even though in some contexts, like Trump's America or Bolsonaro's Brazil, it may look like the political regime is only able to pursue maximum economic returns, regardless of the social cost, the potential for political control is always there. The pace can be accelerated or it can be slowed, depending on the balance of social and political power.

There is no clearer example of how the political economy of speed produces ecocidal tendencies than the fate of that ultimate symbol of capitalist luxury, caviar. Black caviar is harvested from the beluga sturgeon, a fish that is now highly endangered. Within a few years of the collapse of the Soviet Union, the entropic shift from a political system that carefully regulated its supply, to a virulent and decentralised system, began to reveal problems in preserving sustainable sources of caviar. The states bordering the Black Sea, a major site for production of black caviar, had previously restricted fishing to ensure that sturgeon stocks were healthy. When the Soviet Union collapsed in 1991, the newly independent states of Azerbaijan, Kazakhstan and Turkmenistan failed to maintain the system of regulation and significantly increased levels of pollution into the Caspian Sea and its rivers. Of course, pollution was not a new problem. Soviet factories and sewage treatment plants had been polluting the Caspian Sea since the 1960s. But the speed and scale of pollution after 1991 rose exponentially. As the journal *Scientific American* noted in 1998: "countless new plants cropping up on the Caspian's shores – 1,200 or more in Kazakstan alone – have made matters much worse. Baku, the capital of Azerbaijan, pumps some 250 to 300 million cubic meters of sewage into the Caspian annually".[28]

This is not to claim that the former Soviet Union had a rationale or sustainable approach to regulating industry. Critics of the Soviet Union always noted that levels of water and air pollution in places rivalled the most advanced capitalist economies, as did the carbon footprint of the Soviet satellite states.[29] Clearly, any industrial system – because all forms of production and transportation are based to some extent upon the exploitation of natural resources – involves the depletion of those resources, the production of waste, and the impact on the natural environment. Industrial processes using other forms of ownership and organisation that are not necessarily "capitalist" have clearly been bad for the environment.

Yet it is clear that the rate of the political economy of speed matters. It matters because governments can and do generally intervene in ways that regulate the speed of production, distribution and consumption. Indeed, this is the importance of the *political* sphere. The rate at which we are destroying the planet is regulated by a process that is still largely determined by politics.

This means two things. First, it means that even if we trusted corporations to change their behaviour, this is only one of many things that need to happen. Corporate capitalism is not a self-contained system; corporations respond to a range of conditions, including regulatory regimes, fluctuations in market price of commodities, labour market conditions, competition, and so on. Environmental degradation occurs because of a combination of things that corporations have control over and things that they don't. Second, the capacity to control this political economy of speed is not beyond us, precisely because it is a *political* economy. Political interventions have the capacity to change things because corporate capitalism is not a self-contained system; the system relies on the support of governments and other public authorities to ensure that it thrives. The capacity to control the corporation may be beyond the capacity of our immediate groups of friends, family or our workmates. But it is not beyond the capacity of government or the demands of popular movements.

The short arm of the law

Most popular campaigns that seek to reverse environmental damage – whether their aims relate to the curbing of greenhouse emissions, CFCs or ensuring offshore oil workers are safe – tend to involve a demand for *legal* limits to be imposed. Put in the terms outlined above, they seek a legal mechanism that slows the pace of the political economy of speed. Indeed, this is precisely the impetus behind the growing movement to demand that ecocide is recognised as a crime in national and international law. We will consider the chances of success for a new offence of ecocide on those terms later in the chapter.

For the time being, let us consider the wider implications of making demands for more legal controls. The first thing to say is that, if they are made on their own terms, demands for more law, or more effective law, present us with a conundrum. If corporations do not readily accept natural limits imposed by geography, by scarcity of materials or by transportation time, why would they be likely to observe a limit in law? This leads directly to a second question: when we do impose stricter legal limits then how can we expect states to enforce them? As we have noted in the preceding discussion, this is a question of political economy.

Take the issue of particulate air pollution, estimated to kill 4 million people each year globally.[30] The international community has negotiated numerous separate treaties that set out the targets to reduce particulate pollution, such as the 1979 UN Convention on Long-range Transboundary Air Pollution.[31] In order for those treaties to be enforced, national governments have to take action. It was pointed out in the introduction to this book that most of this ambient air pollution is produced by corporations. This means that in order to make international treaties workable, some consideration must be given to how regulatory mechanisms might ensure *corporate* compliance. The first problem is that when it comes to enforcement mechanisms, these vary hugely across the world. Even where those mechanisms are strongest, regulatory enforcement remains a gargantuan task. We are dealing with hundreds of thousands of corporations worldwide, some very small and some very large, some that will observe those limits and others that won't. The first dilemma that environmental regulators face, then, is the task of ensuring that legal limits are not breached.

When regulators impose legal limits, corporations may or may not comply. The chances of being caught doing something that the corporation shouldn't, for example cutting corners to risk lives, is largely in the control of the state. States determine how regulatory regimes work: how often a company will be visited and inspected, how its compliance will be checked on an ongoing basis, and how it will it be punished if it breaks the law. However, as we have seen, normally this depends on a very wide range of political and economic conditions, some that states retain direct control of and others – like market price – that states might have considerably less control over.

In recent decades, the balance of political and social power has made it more difficult to enforce environmental law. Since the 1990s, most environmental regulatory authorities have faced tightening budgets and been unable to do a job that was already incredibly complex and difficult.

In the UK there are over 1 million businesses that the UK Environment Agency is charged with regulating. The Agency employs little more than 1,000 frontline officers dedicated to law enforcement across those sectors. This is little more than the number of traffic wardens in London.[32] Yet the task faced by those regulators – to ensure millions of businesses are complying with the law – is Sisyphean. In the UK, the Environment Agency's annual budget is just 0.13% of annual government spending. The UK is not an outlier in this respect. The UK's approach is broadly comparable with other advanced industrial states; its token approach to regulation does not look especially irresponsible.[33] Spending on the US Environmental

Protection Agency (EPA), for example, accounts for just 0.2% of the annual federal budget.[34]

Globally, both budgetary and political pressures on regulatory agencies have certainly intensified since the 2008 financial crisis. The UK Environment Agency has faced more than a 40% cut to its budget in the decade following the crisis, again a feature of advanced economies that is not unique to the UK. Funding for the US EPA, for example, is now at a 40-year low. This is starting from a very low baseline indeed. Unsurprisingly, *The Washington Post* recently reported that the EPA inspections had fallen to their lowest level in a decade.[35] The Trump administration has just introduced a "no surprises policy" that bans EPA inspectors making surprise visits to power, chemical and waste facilities.[36] Corporate managements will be warned in advance, giving them a chance to cover up any legal breaches. This is just one of a steady stream of attacks on the effectiveness of the EPA by a Trump administration obsessed by "burdens on business". On the same day the no surprises policy was announced, the EPA declared its refusal to ban the deadly pesticide chlorpyrifos.[37]

In avoiding the awkward truth of its own ineffectiveness, the UK Environment Agency has sought to deal with its own particular Sisyphean task with some bizarre changes in regulatory policy. The regulator began to commission research in the early 2000s which promoted a strategy of ignoring the largest companies and concentrate on the small ones. Their data calculations told them this was the most scientific approach. Indeed, two of those commissioned researchers argued: "there is little doubt that larger firms have greater incentives and capacities than smaller firms to comply with and go beyond legal requirements".[38] This rationale justified leaving the biggest corporations alone and by 2009 this approach had become established Agency policy.[39] Self-regulation is now the dominant mode of regulation. Regulators increasingly rely on corporations to volunteer information about their own compliance. As we saw in the introduction to this book, this has never worked, even in the case of the most deadly substances. Those same corporations are hardly likely to volunteer information about their day-to-day compliance with environmental law.

What we are describing here, in the context of the UK and the US, is a global regulatory crisis that has been incubating for at least four decades. Since the 1980s, the international financial institutions like the World Bank and the IMF, along with the most powerful national governments have enthusiastically encouraged policies that seek to undermine a whole range of social protections, including environmental regulation. This political strategy, which bemoans regulation as a "burden on business", promotes the privatisation of public services, seeks further restrictions on workers' rights, and encourages the rolling back of a whole array of limits placed on corporations, has become known as neoliberalism. The project to bring market discipline to the public sector on a grand

scale – with its British origins in the Thatcher governments of the 1980s and its US origins in the Reagan
administration – has always contained a militant anti-
state ideology at its core.

Neoliberalism has acted as a major bulwark against
the enforcement of environmental law and against
demands for adequate funding and stronger powers
for regulators everywhere. And it has intensified the
demand on the need for effective regulators. As we
have seen, the regulation of water quality is a primary
function of the UK Environment Agency. But since
the privatisation of water provision in England, it has
been fighting a losing battle on this front. One investigation by the *Financial Times* revealed that most
water companies were failing in their legal responsibility to keep Britain's waterways safe. A particular problem is the failure to control the flow of raw
sewage into public waterways. None of England's
major rivers are safe enough to swim in because of the
risk of people getting sick. And yet, as this investigation caustically observed: "The concerns over river
pollution come at a time when the water industry
is under fire for paying executives and shareholders
lucrative rewards while raising customer bills and
failing to stem leakage".[40]

Some people get sick, some people get a pay rise.
Those two things are not unrelated.

The fate of our regulatory system is one of the great
tragedies of the neoliberal period. The system of environmental protection that began to be erected in the

mid-nineteenth century, and began to look a little more effective in the 1970s, has been completely eroded.[41] Our system of corporate environmental regulation was enervated before it had a fighting chance of success.

Punishment and the corporate veil

It is clear that the pace and intensity of the political economy of speed varies across time, and across different modes of capitalism. And it is clear that in the neoliberal period, there has been a progressive undermining of political controls that can protect our environment. This begs the question, would we be in a better place if neoliberalism had never happened, and if capitalist states had employed different modes of regulation? Would things be any different if corporations were punished more frequently for breaking environmental law? This brings us back to the problem of regulatory permission and the point that the most harmful industrial practices are not illegal in the first place.

Let us imagine for a moment that we had more stringent environmental limits placed on corporations across capitalist states. How would this work? The answer to this question, partly at least, takes us back to our earlier discussion of the corporate veil. For, even if the law was enforced, there is something about the way *corporations* are punished that does not necessarily focus minds in the boardroom. This seems to be the case across the corporate world. The regularity with which the banks are involved in criminal activities that trigger fines worth hundreds of millions of dollars is truly astounding. Yet those fines seem to be having no impact whatsoever. Between 2012 and 2019, all of the major British banks were punished with mega fines on a regular basis, for offences including: the fixing of the bank rates LIBOR (Barclays $440m) and FOREX (RBS $1.3b; Barclays $1.5b; HSBC $618m); for money laundering (HSBC $1.9b); for ripping off customers (HSBC $470m); and for offences related to the financial crash (Barclays $1.4b; RBS $10b). This list only captures the largest fines. The full charge sheet runs to 100s of offences by the banks in the period since the financial crash in 2008.

If banking looks to be a particularly extreme case, there are other sectors in which penalties for criminal breaches and illegalities occur with the same regularity. Illegal price fixing, for example, in the electrical goods, food retail and construction sectors is every bit as routine and normalised. The regulators charged with dealing with those offences also use fines, sometimes very large ones. The strategy does not appear to be working. The record fine for price fixing was $1.92 billion, imposed by the European Commission on 4 electrical goods firms in 2012. In 2018, another 4 electrical goods firms, including one of the firms fined in 2012 were fined $130 million by the Commission for similar offences.

If fines of this scale are not appearing to work against corporations for those offences, how can we expect to protect the environment using the same regulatory tools? After all, BP's Deepwater Horizon catastrophe in 2010 came after a series of very serious offences, including an explosion that killed 15 workers in their Texas refinery in 2005 (which led to a record $50.6m fine), and a series of oil spills in Alaska in 2006 (which led to a $25m fine).

One reason fines might not have had much impact is that when they are put into perspective, even the largest sums tend to represent a fraction of corporate revenues. The Texas refinery fine represented 0.017% of the BP Group's revenue for 2010, the year the fine was levied, and the Alaska fine amounted to around 0.007% of the group's revenue for 2011, the year that it was levied. The bill for Deepwater Horizon was, as the financial press have enthusiastically noted, been absorbed largely by the rise in oil prices between 2016 and 2018.[42]

Those examples alone do not give cause to argue against the use of fines; indeed, more punitive fines may well be more effective. In theory, at least, deterrence can work when applied to corporations precisely for the same reason deterrence doesn't tend to work with individuals. Corporations have teams of accountants and specialists that can predict their chances of getting caught and estimate the consequences for the business. But this ability to plan also means that they can cushion the blow of a fine.

There has been an acceleration in lawsuits related to climate change. A database published and updated by the Columbia Law School contains 1,380 cases of climate change-related civil actions, mostly in the US. Around 90% of those cases were filed between 2009 and 2019.[43] While those cases are being monitored by corporate lawyers, they are not seen as a significant challenge to Big Oil, or any other corporate interests. Of course, cases like this may have an impact cumulatively or in extreme cases. An analysis in the *Financial Times* has proposed that the class action for Monsanto's Roundup (see the introduction) has reduced the value of Bayer's shares by around a third.[44]

Corporations generally have ways and means to offset such losses. They very often keep slush funds to offset fines and claims. In some cases, they structure their tax in ways that allow them to write off fines! BP received a $10 billion tax rebate by offsetting its Gulf oil spill disaster expenses against tax. As one US campaign group noted, the sum added up to roughly half the size of the $20 billion restitution fund that the company established.[45] Infamously, Exxon had also used tax deductions to ensure that it only paid a fraction of its $1.1 billion settlement for the Valdez oil spill in Alaska in 1989.[46]

For reasons outlined in chapter 1, it may be that even if they were not permitted to offset the costs of fines against reserves or tax, or pass on the costs in other ways, punishing the corporation will never have a deterrent effect no matter how severe the punishment. To repeat the argument developed in chapter 1, punishing the corporation ultimately protects shareholders and senior managers because they remain protected, behind the corporate veil. As the international law scholar Grietje Baars puts it, executives can always say: "It's not me, it's the corporation!"[47]

As we saw in chapter 1, executives occasionally appear in court, but owners and shareholders are rarely even identified in such cases. Fines imposed on companies, for all of the reasons outlined here, have little more effect than perpetuating a structure of power that is ultimately designed to shield class interests. Little wonder then that studies on the impact of pecuniary penalties on the corporation generally find little correlation between the imposition of fines and a deterrent effect.[48]

Conversely, it is the most vulnerable groups of people that will tend to bear the costs of fines. Because fines are generally levied on the "corporation", rather than targeted at a particular group within it, the cost burden of even the largest fine can be absorbed and redistributed; those costs might be offset against a particular budget heading (they might result in cuts to wages or other operational costs), or they may be passed onto customers and clients in the form of price rises, or onto suppliers by reducing the market value of a product. Fines for violating safety laws and causing fatalities in the workplace are often absorbed by workers in the form of wage cuts and downsizing.[49]

The same effect occurs if a corporation is liquidated: the groups that are most likely to absorb the environmental costs of liquidation are local communities who are left to pay for any clean-up. Often liquidation is used strategically to avoid the costs of paying damages. International lawyer Sara L. Seck has identified a number of cases involving US and Canadian firms that conveniently avoided clean-up costs of mines by using a subsidiary and then filing for bankruptcy.[50]

The corporate veil is working well to protect both the senior officers of corporations that take the decisions and the investors who ultimately benefit from those decisions. This leads us directly to another "even if ... " set of questions. Let us assume that our system of punishment was more effective, and that we were able to prosecute investors and senior managers for an offence like ecocide. Our next problem would be whether an offence of ecocide, even if it were it to be effectively prohibited, would be enough to stem global warming and to make a significant impact on levels of pollution.

Regulation at the end-point of the earth

This problem is brought into relief most clearly when we consider that regulatory controls always chose the least invasive point at which to intervene in the industrial cycle. In most capitalist states, most industrial processes are controlled at the end-point. That is to say, the greatest effort that is spent *controlling* greenhouse gases, poisonous substance and harmful waste products happens at the end of the line. The focus of most control systems is the point at which those harmful substances have already been produced, or the point at which harmful production process are already underway.

Controls on emissions are exactly that: controls on the system's harmful outputs. We rarely contemplate this. We rarely question why we don't control the start-point. Occasionally states ban or place restrictive limits on particular substances. But generally, controls placed on even the most harmful substances are imposed when it is too late. The most pressing problem we have with the system of environmental regulation, certainly in advanced capitalist states, is that it barely regulates the damage we are doing to our planet at all. Indeed the particular mode of control adopted in capitalist regulatory systems is based on the assumption that the brakes can only be applied after the damage has been done. I call this mode of control "end-point regulation".

In the rare cases that companies are prosecuted for offences, it is at the very end-point of production and distribution that chemicals, oil, plastic products and so on are controlled. The same goes for international efforts to control greenhouse gases and other pollutants. The regulation of oil, coal and gas and other carbon fuels, for example, tends to be regulated at the very end-point in the life cycle of those products. There is a certain logic to this. It is carbon emissions that are bringing us to the point of climate catastrophe. Yet, once the oil or coal is out of the ground, it will be sold and used unless its sale and use is banned or severely controlled. End-point control is the dominant approach taken in the main treaties and targets that seek to reverse the crisis. The solutions offered are the control of *emissions* rather than the control of how substances are produced in the first place.

Our failure to intervene and limit the damage done by the production of carbon dioxide, by other poisons and by waste is partly due to how we regulate. As the argument in the previous chapter outlined, the regulation of pollution and other forms of environmental damage has the simultaneous aim of *controlling* the corporation and *permitting* the corporation to continue polluting (within some limits of course). In the context of the Kyoto and the Paris agreements (and the carbon trading method for meeting its targets) this balancing act can only be achieved when regulation takes place after carbon minerals are already out of the ground – after the fossil fuels have already been extracted. Indeed, almost all other treaties that seek to limit waste and pollution and protect biodiversity use a similar approach – to impose limits at the end point of production. The tendency is to place general limits on emissions, creating new laws about the use of products that have already been made; or to identify particular geographical areas for protection from substances that are already in circulation. And this is the point about the crime of "ecocide". If ecocide does become legitimised – and even enforced – as a crime in international law, it may well prove to be an important recognition that the destruction of the planet must be taken seriously. However, as we saw in the previous chapter, this is not what law – certainly not criminal law – does in capitalist societies. Even the strongest forms of legal intervention allow the state to absorb conflicts in ways that preserve the autonomy of corporations, and therefore preserve the ability of the people who hide behind the corporation to commit ecocide!

The general impetus in capitalist forms of legal regulation is precisely this: to enable the rich to pursue their own interests, no matter the social consequences. And this is the real reason that regulation always comes too late to make a difference; this is why the state largely limits the scope of its intervention to the end point of the production process. A report by oil and gas consultancy Wood MacKenzie estimates that if we maintain the current rate of energy transition, coal, oil and gas will still contribute about 85% of the world's primary energy supply by 2040, compared with 90% today.[51] The major oil companies continue to spend little over 1% of revenue on the development of renewables.[52] Such projections make a mockery of the targets set by the Paris Accord. This is one indication that the system shows no signs of taking the crisis seriously. The preferred mode of end-point control will never really be effective in preventing ecocidal production in any meaningful sense.

Yet it is the principle of end-point control that dominates the mechanisms that are introduced ostensibly to control climate change. "Carbon trading" is the name given to the allocative market mechanism that was first put in place by the Kyoto treaty. In this system, a nation or a major corporate polluter can buy a permit to emit more; nations with fewer emissions can sell their permit to other countries or corporations. Lauded as a revolutionary method of reducing emissions, it mimicked a number of proposals economists have made over the years that use market logic to deal with externalities.[53]

The idea is that carbon trading enables the nations and corporations that emit more carbon dioxide to "meet" carbon emission targets by offsetting against those that emit less. The main criticism of this system is that it simply perpetuates a process in which the largest polluters are able to maintain high levels of pollution because they can afford to pay for it. The system also contains other in-built incentives to pollute. Because credits can be allocated to companies that are very high polluters but make some improvement to reduce carbon emissions; very often the largest polluters are allocated the most permits. As journalist Naomi Klein has noted, some of the biggest polluting corporations in India and China install relatively cheap "green" technologies that remove some greenhouse gases but are still highly resource intensive. They then reap millions of dollars worth of carbon credits at a relatively low cost to them.[54] They may even use this credit to maintain high carbon emissions at another facility. It is also likely that, between nations, the export of coal and high-carbon oil and gas from the Global North to the Global South is a market that is *encouraged* by carbon credits. In other words, there is a continued tolerance of carbon emissions built into this system. Moreover, because the number of projects obtaining carbon credits is rapidly growing, this is an expanding market that is liable to multiply both the benefits and the counter-productive effects of the system. It is a naïve and entirely wrong logic that says by controlling demand, supply will sort itself out. Indeed, it is a repetition of the same market logic that has brought us to this point.

Carbon trading is end-point regulation *par excellence*. It avoids all of the most pressing questions that need to be answered if we are to do something about climate change. Why can carbon fuels not be cut off at source? Why can they not be phased out by controlling their production? The most basic answer is that this is the very antithesis of a market logic which endlessly claims that market mechanisms are the solution to all of our problems, even when the problems have been created in the market in the first place!

And this brings us back to the corporation. As we saw in chapters 1 and 2, the corporation's primary function is to reproduce capital. It does this by providing the vehicle through which most capital is invested. Intervention at the end point of the investment cycle is the least intrusive point for the corporate model. On the other hand, when we intervene at the start-point, this means intervening much more directly against investors and therefore corporations. It means intervening to control the extraction of raw materials, intervening in chemical and other industrial manufacturing processes. And it also means intervening to control the financing of corporate activities. Intervening at the start-point as well as the end point in the production cycle means fundamentally changing the financial model that is the major driving force of corporate ecocide.

Conclusion

As this chapter has argued, regulators in capitalist societies have a dual function. On one hand, their function demands the promotion of a political economy of speed that prioritises economic growth, and on the other hand, states are responsible for activities that are harmful to the environment. It is this contradiction that makes some people pessimistic about our reliance on states to protect us. Indeed in the commentary to Falk's original 1973 formulation of the crime of ecocide he makes a declaration that: "the State system is inherently incapable of organizing the defence of the planet against ecological destruction".[55] Falk questions, as we must, how capable our regulatory system could ever be in preventing ecocide. Our discussion of the way that states regulate corporations in capitalist societies forces us to ask this question again and again.

The regulation of ecocide in a serious way requires that we control the start-point of production and the distribution of things – not just that we tinker with the speed of the political economy. To have a crime of ecocide on the statute books would only be significant if it was accompanied by the control or banning of the full range of commercial activities that are currently licenced. But even then, a series of prosecutions against senior individuals or indeed a corporation itself is not going to precipitate a shift the structure of the economic system that we need. This is largely because, as we saw in chapter 1, the corporate structure is purpose-built to ensure that the people who profit the most are shielded from bearing the environmental costs of corporate activities.

Yet to argue that the system must change does not mean arguing that regulation is pointless. This can never be an "all or nothing" discussion. There is a well-worn debate in left-wing politics between revolutionary and reformist positions. This is always a false opposition. When we seek radical social change, we are never given a simplified choice of reform or revolution, with nothing in between. Governments need to slow the pace and intensity of the political economy of speed now more than ever before. Yet, at the same time, in order to confront the realities of the problem that we face we need to recognise that the 'end-point' approach to regulation ultimately sustains the nature-devouring corporate economy, albeit in a less aggressive and more 'green' form.

As we saw in the previous chapter, corporations do not respect the human or moral limits placed on their activities. When we talk about legal limits, as we have done in this chapter, we are introducing a different type of limit. It is not physical in the sense that it does not involve limits on the availability of raw materials, or the time taken to transport goods, for example. Legal limits are imposed externally, by political authorities (governments, law courts, regulatory authorities, international organisations). As eco-socialist Joel Kovel has argued, "there are no internal limits to the expansion of capitalist production".[56] This is why limits must be imposed on corporations by regulators. At the same time, as this chapter has shown, regulatory systems established for dealing with climate change and ecocide have very often proven to be counter-productive: regulatory solutions very often encourage the planet-destroying practices they claim to be able to stop.

The regulatory approach to ecocide is not working and it must be changed. If we are to demand "more regulation" and "more prosecution" for ecocide in the aftermath of capitalism's crises, then we need to be sure that we are not merely strengthening the institutional forms of power that created the crisis in the first place. We need a form of regulatory intervention that can secure a lasting solution to the crisis; such approaches to regulation must ensure that corporate structures are not merely reproduced or strengthened. Otherwise, we will simply be reproducing the conditions that are killing us. The following chapter – the conclusion to this book – begins to set out the ways that we might go about this task.

Conclusion: kill the corporation before it kills us

How long can history keep repeating itself?

The Stora Enso story, which has featured as our point of departure in each chapter, reveals the remarkable endurance of the corporation throughout history. Indeed, as a structure through which profits can be reproduced, it has proven to be more sustainable than the resources and the land it has devoured and replenished. If the land around Falun remains barren, the land in its plantations in Uruguay and Rio Grande do Sul may well be very soon, as a result of the monocultural plantations that exhaust the soil of their nutrients. In Northern Europe there are signs that this history will repeat itself. The logging of Swedish forests by Stora Enso and other European wood companies has drastically impacted upon the biodiversity of those forests, and has led to an ongoing loss of species that are essential to protecting the sustainability of those habitats. The Swedish Society for Nature Conservation noted in 2009:

> in the counties of Jämtland, Dalarna and Värmland, SSNC has discovered a remarkable number of forests containing key habitats that Stora Enso has notified

for final felling. The planning of these loggings demonstrate a lack of consideration of high nature values and a poor capacity to identify key habitats.[1]

The dormant Falun copper mine is also in Dalarna County. History repeats itself indeed!

Almost all of the oil, chemical, mining and manufacturing corporations referred to in the introduction to this book are still making and selling deadly products. At the same time, these companies are still commissioning research, muddying the waters, creating doubt and blaming someone else. Indeed, most of those corporations continue to profit and thrive.[2] Of course, those two things are not unrelated.

Fifty years after the ecocidal use of Agent Orange in the Vietnam war, Monsanto retains a powerful presence in the country. It is the biggest importer of genetically modified organisms (GMOs) to Vietnam. Although a deal with the Vietnamese government has meant that it is officially encouraged in this enterprise, there are big questions about the long-term impact of GMOs, not least their in-bred resistance to chemicals such as Roundup (see chapter 2). GMOs facilitate the aggressive commodification of seeds, privatise varieties that were previously commonly owned, and therefore expand corporate control over food supplies.[3] The result is that local farmers are either forced off the land or forced to use Monsanto varieties. At the same time, Monsanto's GMOs are designed to be used in conjunction with some very damaging chemicals.

One of the major claims made about GMOs is that they can deal with extreme climate change conditions, such as drought. The development of "climate-ready" crops has been controlled by a small number of very powerful players. Six corporations – DuPont, BASF, Syngenta, Bayer, Dow and, of course, Monsanto – control 77% of the patents on those crops.[4] This cycle of corporate pollution/corporate solution gives us a glimpse of our immediate future.

In all of the major industries implicated in the eco-crisis, corporations have already begun to plan for a profitable climate change. This cycle of corporate pollution/corporate solution that is repeating itself around the world gives us a glimpse of our immediate future. If we are not careful, and if we do not wrestle control of our economy and our society from corporate capitalism, then all we will be left with are solutions that someone can make a profit from. As Karl Marx famously said, paraphrasing the German philosopher Georg Hegel, "history repeats itself; the first time as tragedy, the second time as farce".[5] On this count he was probably over-simplifying things. Rather than a process of simple repetition, it might now be more accurate to describe the condition of history as an endless cycle of ecological tragedy. History repeats itself, he might have said today, the first time as tragedy, the second time to make a profit from the tragedy, and the third time, and the fourth time.

The Anthropocene[6] may well be the stage in human

history at which this cycle stops abruptly, simply because there will be no human history left to repeat.

Green market fetishism

Big Oil's strategy has been to play down the scale of the problem and argue strongly against regulatory controls that put the planet before profit. Research published in 2019 by the NGO InfluenceMap revealed that the five largest oil and gas corporations (ExxonMobil, Royal Dutch Shell, Chevron, BP and Total) had invested over $1 billion in misleading climate-related branding and lobbying since the Paris Agreement was signed. Over $200 million of this was used directly to control, delay or block binding policy on climate change.[7]

Yet this strategy of greenwashing in its crudest form is not sustainable.[8] The fossil fuel industry can no longer credibly claim, as it has in the past, that climate change is a bogus science. Yet it continues to double down behind the scenes to preserve the long-term future of fossil fuels. The only alternative it has is to embark on a major rebranding that ultimately seeks to transform Big Oil's reputation from destroyers of the planet to saviours of the planet. ExxonMobil has pledged $100 million for emissions-reduction research[9] (2 months after BP pledged exactly the same thing).[10] All of the oil majors are claiming to be moving towards a sustainable business model. However, if we look at what this means in real terms, it does not look like there is much of a shift away from fossil fuels at all.

BP is pledged to "flat-line" its carbon emissions up to 2025;[11] and Shell has set a target of 20% net reduction in its carbon emissions before 2035.[12] For these companies, any marginal reductions will be achieved by investing more heavily in less carbon-rich gas, rather than a significant switch to renewables.

If the greening of Big Oil smacks of a damage limitation exercise, then, we might ask, what type of damage is it seeking to limit? When the Paris Agreement was being drawn up, it was estimated that in order to reach its targets, Big Oil would be prohibited from exploiting 30% of known oil reserves and 50% of known gas reserves. The oil companies would also need to abandon all exploration and drilling in the Arctic.[13] Perhaps more significantly, their shareholders would take a major hit on dividends that remain the biggest in the corporate world.[14]

At the same time, a great deal of work is going into planning, not to save the world, but to meander into an era of climate breakdown. According to the financial projections made by BP and Shell, their respective business models assume continued profitability in a scenario of a 5°C increase in global temperatures.[15] By the way, this is an increase that most scientists assume will kill millions, if not billions of people. As Mark Lynas has argued, at 5°C hotter, all of the scientific evidence suggests "an entirely new planet is coming into being – one unrecognizable from the one we know today".[16] Even after all of the struggles over climate change, and even after all of those corporations' public commitments, they are still planning to profit as the world collapses around them. They are planning a future in which the oil companies can survive longer than us! This is galling enough, but BP and Shell have more control over the situation than almost any other organisation.

This sort of tinkering at the margins of an over-heating world is all the corporate sector seems ready to offer. Companies like MacDonalds, KFC and Starbucks[17] are pumping millions into developing sustainable packaging. Yet, as long as they continue to make billions from business models that demand expansion into markets that source meat, soya and coffee from some of the world's most ecologically vulnerable regions, this is mere tinkering. While it clearly is a token effort in terms of its real impact on environmental sustainability, initiatives like this mean something much bigger to those companies; they allow a message to be projected to customers who want to buy into "green" brands.

There is no doubt about it, we are in an era of green market fetishism[18] in which ecocide, just like any other human crisis, can be turned into a business opportunity. Because of our reliance on corporations to provide all of our basic goods and services, and because of the control that corporations exert over markets, climate change can be highly profitable.

The following (genuine) statement was broadcast on Bloomberg News in late 2018:

> The rights to pollute the atmosphere with carbon dioxide raced through 25 euros per ton and are now trading at their highest level in a decade. Options data shows that traders are making bigger and bigger bets on prices at or above 30 euros in 2019 already.[19]

Throwaway investment advice like this is issued every day in the financial press; daily feeds tell us how buoyant markets in pollution are. Few would disagree that financial trading in carbon derivatives is not only tasteless, but that it inserts risk into a system that cannot bear any more risk. In the previous chapter it was argued that the system of carbon trading contains a series of built-in incentives that, under some circumstances, can encourage the production of more rather than less carbon dioxide. Derivatives markets in carbon trading at their best have a neutral impact, and at their worst make the eco-system more vulnerable to fluctuations in financial markets.

In recent years there has been a rapid growth in climate change investment funds. Deutsche Bank's *DWS Climate Change Fund* channels investment into the Big Agri climate-ready crops, into water treatment and desalination via water supply firms like Veolia and the Chinese Duoyuan Global Water, and fertiliser multinationals like Yara and Agrium.[20] Those investment funds are creating new markets for those who want to profit from climate change without actually tackling the causes.

Other climate change investment funds are geared up even more explicitly to profiteering from climate change. The Schroder Global Climate Change Fund invests massively in farmland in areas least likely to be affected by global warming, and in food companies and supermarkets, to take advantage of the coming food crisis.[21] There is also a steady growth in the markets of private logistic and security companies specialising in disaster response;[22] and firms that profit from both rebuilding and insuring the infrastructure. And so it goes, on and on, the endless cycle of corporate pollution/corporate solution.

The lesson of history, however, is that corporations will fight tooth and nail to defend their right to make a profit even if it is killing us. It is clear that the only way to break this cycle of corporate pollution/corporate solution is to break the corporation itself. Drastic problems need drastic solutions.

The lightbulb moment

As this book was being written, the global supermarket chain Aldi made an announcement that it planned to trial a change in the packaging of its 4-packs of toilet rolls. Instead of plastic, Aldi was preparing to pack its (bleached) toilet rolls in recyclable paper. But only as a trial. And, it announced, it would only switch permanently to this "new" method of packaging if it was successful. The ocean is filling up with plastic, landfill is bursting at the seams, and one supermarket is only going to cut down on one variety of its batch packaging if "it is successful"![23] So what measure of success do supermarkets like Aldi need? In the super-market business, success of a trial invariably means it receives good feedback from customer surveys and focus groups.

Despite everyone knowing that the system is set up to deflect responsibility onto us as individuals for things we are not actually in control of and that this will not be enough to bring us back from the brink of ecological collapse, the deflection of responsibility onto consumers remains *the* mode of our supposed great transformation.

The futility of individualised, consumer solutions is perhaps best summed up, inadvertently, in the ground-breaking film on climate change, *An Inconvenient Truth*. For many people this was a lightbulb moment, a realisation that we might have gone too far, that the earth was either reaching tipping point, or was too far gone. By the end of the film, desperate to know what we need to do to reverse global warming, we are told to fill our kettle a little less and plant trees, use more energy efficient light bulbs, the usual stuff. And at one point, the film informs us that, if we believe in prayer, we should pray. This was not the kind of lightbulb moment those of us who saw the film were looking for.

Almost 15 years after this film was released to criti-cal acclaim, we remain obsessed with individual solu-tions to the most collective of problems. We find this wholly unsatisfactory approach in the most recent accounts of the climate crisis and what we should do about it. In Martin Dorey's book *No. More. Plastic.*,[24] for example, the author urges his readers to do things like "try using a fountain pen, with real ink, to cut down your pen waste" and "buy [workmates] all a coffee mug and ask them not to bring takeaway cups into the office". Our imaginative capacity for action seems to stop at the feet of individuals.

There is no doubt that, as individuals, all of us need to take action to reduce our carbon footprint. We need to get rid of our cars, to fly less and to buy local food. But there is one reason that this will not be enough to change the system. And it's a very simple reason: we are not in control. As customers, we may be able to protest, and sometimes boycott particular products. But those limited tactics are of little use to us if we do not have any control over the key decisions about how our economy works.

Even if we could assert our power as customers, collectively it would probably add up to less than we think. Remember the research mentioned in the introduction that concluded just 100 companies are responsible for 71% of carbon emissions.[25] Given that much of the remaining 29% will be produced by corporations outside the "top" 100, that doesn't leave us much room to do much as individuals. This is the case even if we were to break it down sector by sector. According to research by Investopedia, the majority of airline revenue comes from commercial customers.[26] And even if we boycotted particular foodstuffs, how could this lead to the change in the system of food production and distribution that we urgently need? There have been points in history at which consumers have been able to exercise power over markets,[27] but only when they have been highly organised collectively. Even when we use our power as consumers collectively, rather than as individuals, in order to be effective we need to be organised as a social movement.

Because they are focussed on changing consumption patterns, individual solutions tend to be based on what is described in the previous chapter as "end-point regulation". When we buy a particular type of lightbulb or pen or cup, make a decision to buy a hybrid vehicle, or even decide to boycott plastic packaging, we are acting as individuals seeking to control an end-point in a cycle of production that has already been completed. Changing the behaviour of individuals is of course crucial in the sense that it changes the aggregate demand for particular products. More dramatic and immediate results will require the control of production and the supply of particular products into the market.

Controlling the start-point

Intervening at the start-point means intervening to control the extraction of raw materials, and to prevent, or at least slow the pace of, the political economy of speed in chemical, agricultural and other industrial processes. It also means intervening to control the *financing* of a large number of environmentally damaging industries. Intervening at the start-point as well as the end point in the production cycle means fundamentally changing the financial model that is the major driving force of climate change. The dominance of corporations over every stage in the industrial process tells us that if we want to intervene at the start-point, this means intervening against corporations.

A movement to ban CFCs in 1999 (as we saw in the introduction to this book) was successful in the face of the determined opposition of two of the world's most powerful corporations. Although a global ban on asbestos has not quite been achieved, the export of asbestos to countries like Bangladesh and India is only possible because of the failure to challenge the power of Canadian and Russian asbestos corporations.

By the time this book is in print, a ban on plastic straws, stirrers and cotton buds will be in force across the UK. Those are important initiatives, but they are very small steps. Plastic straws are estimated to add up to 0.02% of total global plastic waste every year.[28] If a plastic ban is to be effective, it must cover a much more significant proportion of the plastics market. Contrast this ban with the approach taken on plastic bags for example. In 2015, a European Union directive prohibited the free distribution of plastic carrier bags in retail stores. Carrier bags were subjected to a new minimum charge of 5p per bag. This charge was levied not on the companies that had for years produced and distributed plastic bags, but on customers. By all accounts it has had some impact. Three years after the ban, it had claimed to reduce plastic bag littering by 30%. Yet there is still a huge market in plastic bags, and a much larger market in the production of packaging. According to Greenpeace, Britain's supermarkets alone create more than 800,000 tonnes of plastic packaging waste every year.[29]

In 2007, the President of Ecuador, Rafael Correa, offered a slightly different form of carbon trading deal. He promised not to drill for oil in a pristine area of the Amazon forest in the country's Yasuni National Park. The oil would be left under the forest in return for compensation of $3.6 billion from the international community (or roughly half of the revenue the government could expect from the oil). By 2013 international donations had only yielded a fraction of what Correa had asked for – around 0.36% – and drilling began in Yasuni in 2016.[30] Correa has disappointed many of his supporters. Yet his attempt at a moratorium was itself an acknowledgement that effective regulation means stopping production before it goes ahead.

The fact that around 100 companies are responsible for 71% of global carbon production in the past 30 years makes the political task of fixing things look deceptively simple. And at one level it is. Our foremost demand should be the immediate sequestration of all assets of those companies, placed under public control. But even this radical measure would not entirely solve the problem. When counted a different way, a very broad range of corporations are involved in significant carbon emissions. Research by the think tank Green Alliance shows that inefficiencies in production, and the generation of waste across the construction, food, clothing and electronics industries, account for half of Britain's CO_2 emissions.[31]

In short, controlling the start point is necessary, but it is only a piecemeal solution. As long as they remain the principal organisations responsible for making, consuming and distributing things, corporations remain in control of industrial processes and the way they are financed. The fix to the mess we are in cannot possibly be provided by organisations that are programmed to devour nature, with no regard for the human and ecological consequences. The fix must be political.

A green industrial revolution?

The introduction to this book noted that in most of the political proposals for a "green new deal" and a "green industrial revolution", the corporation is rarely discussed explicitly as a problem that needs to be confronted head-on. Yet it is obvious that many of the proposals and the blueprints for a green new deal would effectively mean limiting the power and the economic role of profit-making corporations across the economy, not just those in the energy and fossil fuel industry. At a very minimum, we need to see the introduction of two types of tax on corporations (a carbon tax, and a financial transaction tax), and they would need to be introduced on a global scale. But even this would only be a start. The task we have ahead of us is huge. We need to phase out all carbon fuels, plastics and an almost unfathomable range of chemical substances that are ubiquitous in industry. We need to localise food and manufacturing, and introduce revolutionary methods of cutting waste.

Some proposals have demanded wholesale reconstruction of the financial system,[32] and often involve the nationalisation of transport companies, the creation of new forms of recycling cooperatives, models of constitutive decision-making and new modes of "slow" and "local" food production.[33] Alexandria Ocasio-Cortez's proposals contain some mix of these policies. Taken together, they would represent a profound challenge to the model of corporate capitalism that currently dominates our lives. However, it is unclear how this task might be achieved. Nor is it exactly clear what would be needed to ensure that the economy would no longer be dominated by profit-making, share-owned corporations.

Of course, this task is made more difficult by the fact that the executives of the corporations most implicated in all of this are routinely appointed to government positions, asked to advise on regulatory policy, or access politics in other ways through political donations and lobbying.[34] Ending the political input of corporations into green new deal policies might be difficult, but would be a pre-requisite for getting the job done. In order to complete the gargantuan task of transforming dirty jobs into clean jobs, there will need to be social upheaval on a scale never seen before. Some very powerful vested interests are going to lose a lot in a "just transition" from the corporate economy. This is why any effective measures will require a sustained struggle outside as well as inside government. Corporate elites will resist, and we must prepare to organise against them.

As we saw in chapter 1, a fledgling corporate social responsibility movement in the 1930s proposed changes in law that could promote "director primacy" rather than shareholder primacy. A version of this was introduced by the UK Companies Act 2006. Indeed, it is becoming much more prevalent for capitalist democracies to develop proposals that enable directors to take into account the interests of a wider group of stakeholders.[35] The problem with these proposals is that they virtually always strengthen, rather than weaken, the ironclad rule of shareholder primacy. Since its implementation in 2007, the UK Companies Act has made virtually no difference to corporate governance, except to give corporate and NGO lawyers something else to argue about.

Of course, as we saw in chapter 3, the function of law in capitalist societies is to keep the ship steady and make sure the corporation is not impeded too much as it goes about its business. A green new deal will not come to be introduced as part of a consensual process. It is unlikely that legislators will be allowed to transform the economy whilst the most powerful sections of the leading economies just sit back and watch in despair. A green new deal will need its own sources of social power. This means that it will need a sustained popular movement behind it, agitating for and demanding radical social change every step of the way.

Ecocide or the corporate death penalty?

As Richard Falk, author of the draft law of ecocide, argued, we have good reason to be sceptical about how capable a state-administered regulatory system will be in preventing ecocide. Of course, Falk's answer lay in international rather than national law; in international criminal prosecutions rather than national regulatory systems. The proponents of a law of ecocide have argued that the chances of ending up in the International Criminal Court (ICC) will focus minds in the boardrooms. It is difficult to argue with the proposition that the threat of prosecution for destroying the environment is probably better than no threat at all. However, as other critics of the ICC have noted, the chances of ending up in the dock at the Hague are roughly zero, unless you are African and unless you are on the wrong side of a civil war. This is not just invective: in the first decade of the ICC's operation, only Africans had been brought to trial.[36]

But let us say, for argument's sake, that ecocide breaks the mould: that this is the offence that will enable white people from Western Europe and Australia and North America to be prosecuted at the ICC. Even if there were a handful of prosecutions for ecocide, we are still left with all the problems identified in the previous chapter. The chances of individual directors being held accountable would still be almost negligible. While at the same time, investors shareholders and owners would remain untouchable.

A new offence of ecocide may therefore present a false symbolic hope that the international community will act, whilst at the same time simply providing a way of side-lining the issue into a few "monster" cases and allowing the problem to be left in the hands of cause-lawyer firms and the ICC.[37] Law, if it serves a function at all in dealing with ongoing ecocide, is always going to fall short as *the* solution. A more complex problem here is that any reforms to international *criminal* law will not break the enduring and over-arching structure of *corporate* law. No matter how well the law is enforced and no matter how harsh the penalties, criminal law can only offer highly individualised solutions that focus on a few "bad apples", or, as we found in the previous chapter, solutions that keep the investment and financial structure of corporations intact.

One of the more radical strands of argument in the research dealing with corporate crime is a resurgence of the idea of the "corporate death penalty". US legal theorists Mary and Steven Ramirez have proposed to formalise a corporate death penalty based on a version of "three strikes and you're out", the policy notoriously used by the US and other states from the 1980s onwards to deal with relatively petty offending.[38] Instead of going to jail, the "out" would be that the corporation would be "put to death", or put into liquidation by the courts after a third serious offence.

One problem with this proposal is that the courts in many jurisdictions already have this option available, and are afraid to use it. Since 2015 in England and Wales, for example, the courts have been empowered to impose unlimited fines for environmental and health and safety offences. Theoretically at least, a large enough fine can immediately divest a corporation of all of its assets, thus effectively putting it into liquidation.[39] This, however, is yet to happen. The same effect follows when unusually high civil damages are imposed.

A second problem that lies not in law, but in the corporate structure, makes this "corporate death penalty" seem highly counter-productive. As we saw in the previous chapter, when companies are forced into liquidation, the costs of collapse are borne by workers and communities, and indeed severely reduce the possibility of an environmental clean-up. The fate of the pensions of people who worked for the asbestos UK firm Turner and Newall is a particularly tragic one. In 2001, Federal-Mogul, the US asbestos firm, and owners of Turner and Newall, went bankrupt and left a pension fund deficit of around £400 million. This pension fund affected a group of people that were already facing a slow and painful death due to asbestos exposure. As well as having profound impacts on workers, bankruptcy often also prevents communities gaining compensation or damages. This happened when US corporation Pacific Gas and Electricity filed for bankruptcy and thus instantly avoided the consequences of libel action for its failure to prevent wildfires in California in 2017 and 2018.

Compensation for causing externalities (as we have seen, the "third party" environmental costs that corporations will never have to pay for) and the costs of restitution (or clean-up costs) are barely recognised in bankruptcy law. Yet even if they were, this would not prevent exactly the same thing happening again. When corporations are involved in environmental catastrophes, investors and company directors are permitted either to continue to profit within a variation of the same corporate structures, or to move on to the next corporation to invest in or to work for. The "corporate death penalty", in the form proposed by Mary and Steven Ramirez is not really a corporate death penalty at all. It is a licence for the most powerful people within the corporation to continue what they are doing after the company is liquidated.

This is not to say that the general point made by the proposers of the corporate death penalty is not worth pursuing. We should recall that a significant radical demand in response to the financial crisis was that the banks should no longer be allowed to operate in the same way. Many argued that we should simply bring the banks into public ownership with minimal compensation for shareholders. Indeed, in some jurisdictions something like this actually happened. Yet the model of public ownership in the places where there was a bank bailout, comprised of a token restructuring which put the interests of the largest investors before the public interest. For example, as part of the bailout deal, the British government wholly acquired RBS. This "public" ownership has not altered the management of the bank substantially, but in order to protect shareholders, the government has been the guarantor of the bank's liquidity until the point it will be handed back to private investors. The net loss to taxpayers of this strategy has been estimated to add up to £26 billion.[40]

The COVID-19 pandemic and the 2008 global financial crisis should have been our real lightbulb moments. They should have been the moments that we realised how easy it would be to establish another financial system. They could have been the points at which a more sustainable economy was born. Indeed, there was a proposal for a green new deal published in 2008. As one of the authors, Ann Pettifor, has recalled, those proposals began to gain political traction before it all got eclipsed by the chaotic aftermath of the Lehman Brothers bankruptcy. Instead of thinking through lasting, sustainable solutions to the financial crisis, the politicians did what they always do: they left the control of the economy in the hands of the banks and corporate elites.

It is easy to read history in hindsight. At the same

time the only way to save the planet may be to heed the lessons of our recent history. One consequence of the growing movement against climate change is that when another financial crash of this magnitude comes, as it almost certainly will, there will be an even bigger critical mass demanding alternatives to our unsustainable economy.

Breaking the structure of corporate power

Unless decisive change is forced upon them, investors and senior managers will continue to use corporations to do exactly the same things they have been doing for more than four centuries. Decisive change must involve a root and branch deconstruction of the corporate structure itself. No matter the apparent impossibility of this task, there are some very clear conclusions we can draw from the analysis set out in this book. Three ways in which effective structural change might be achieved are summarised below.

1. The corporate structure must be broken

As a number of contemporary corporate theorists have argued, early "fictional entity" theories (see chapter 1) can be invoked to restore the corporate charter as the legal authority for restricting the scope of corporate activities. Academics such as Joel Bakan[41] and David Ciepley[42] argue that this would enable states to prevent corporations from doing particular things and from expanding their sphere of influence. A similar, and disarmingly simple, solution proposed by Indian writer and activist Arundhati Roy is to abolish cross-ownership in business so that

> weapons manufacturers cannot own TV stations, mining corporations cannot run newspapers, business houses cannot fund universities, drug companies cannot control public health funds.[43]

The advantage of such proposals to limit the scope of what a corporation can and cannot do is that they offer a way of radically limiting the ability of capital to reproduce itself. However, even if we were to achieve this kind of restructure of corporate capitalism, we would still have to deal with the structural impetus towards environmental destruction that exists as part of the corporation's DNA, even the "single purpose corporation".

The scope of the corporation has few limits measured either in geographical terms or in terms of its purpose. As we saw in chapter 1, corporations are relatively privileged in so far as they are permitted to cross borders and operate across national jurisdictions. Those privileges, along with the immense economic power corporations enjoy, combine to create the driving force behind the most environmentally destructive processes. Neo-colonial relationships are facilitated hugely by the ability of corporations to create multiple identities and operate through secrecy jurisdictions or "tax havens".

The only way to deal with such privileges is to restrict the global scope of corporations. This would

mean preventing corporations having complex ownership structures by incorporating in multiple jurisdictions and exploiting complex chains of subsidiaries.

All of this seems rather speculative, given the
immense size and reach of global corporations right
now, and it would need an international treaty that
is enforceable and is enforced. Speculative, perhaps,
but not entirely unimaginable. There is a global treaty
on the harmful impact of transnational corporations
currently being negotiated in the UN Human Rights
Council.[44] While there is nothing currently on the
agenda about changing the global *structure* of corporations, we will not be able to ignore the need to tackle
the basic architecture of capitalism for much longer.

2. Impunity for investors and shareholders must end

The principle of limited liability is unsustainable.
Those who own shares in a company, or those with
any type of ownership for that matter, should be held
liable for *all* of the damages caused by the corporation.

This means that shareholders, owners and other
types of investors should be fully responsible for the
damages caused by the activities they profit from, not
merely those that are fixed by regulatory fines or damages fixed in tort law and in civil cases. Shareholders
and owners should be automatically responsible for all
of the health costs and the clean-up costs associated
with their investments. This may seem like an
obvious, fair and equitable proposal. But in practice it

may prove difficult to count those costs directly; and indirect costs will need to be given a notional value, linked to the costs of transition from a carbon-based economy, and the costs of restoring land, air and water quality.

This seismic shift in our standard ways of counting things will need an army of new environmental accountants marching to a new tune – accountants outside the corporate world. Yet it is not beyond us. As critical accountant Prem Sikka has noted, there are currently 350,000 professionally qualified accountants in the UK. Most of them are corporate accountants. We therefore have the resources and could re-direct their efforts and expertise towards socially useful purposes relatively painlessly.

The related principle of asset shielding (see chapter 1) is just as pernicious as the principle of limited liability. We should no longer tolerate the corporate shareholder, like UK industrialist Philip Green, who allegedly used corporate structures to protect all of his homes and $175m yacht as his employees lost their jobs and their pensions.[45] Indeed, as this book was being completed, a total of 6 US coalmining companies reported that they were filing for bankruptcy, thus putting the health care plans and pensions of 100,000 miners at risk, whilst at the same time executives continued to claim remuneration, safe in the knowledge that their personal assets remained protected.[46]

There is an important but little-known body of research that develops a radical idea for dealing with corporate crime. This research proposes a system known as equity fines for ensuring that shareholders and investors pay for the damage that is caused by the things they profit from.[47] The basic idea of equity fines is that a proportion of the shareholding is issued to a group of workers, to the community or to a public body as a way of seeking compensation directly from the shareholders or owners. When this happens, a proportion of the business is effectively re-socialised, reducing the value of other shareholdings. In other words, equity fines reclaim value directly from shareholders through a process of share dilution. The courts, or the administrative authority in this proposal, order the issue of a new batch of shares worth a proportion of the corporation's existing equity. The shares are then controlled by a defined set of fund-holders. The fund could be controlled by a public body, a collective of workers, or the local community. In cases where this is warranted, full ownership of the corporation could be transferred. The equity fine model therefore provides a working basis for a form of the corporate death penalty whereby "death" really means is the forfeiture of class entitlements. After this "death", the corporation can be-reborn under a different form of organisation and different forms of ownership.

3. Impunity for corporate executives must end

If we were to demand that every Big Oil executive was to forfeit all of their assets to contribute to a programme of carbon justice as a matter of policy, without any need for legal proceedings, this would probably be much more effective than the distant threat of a case in the ICC. There is nothing stopping us from doing both. And there is nothing stopping us from reclaiming assets accumulated from those who profit from all environmentally destructive offences. This, after all, is standard practice in the criminal justice system when it comes to other forms of socially damaging markets. Gangsters and corporate fraudsters have their funds and assets sequestrated by the courts routinely. All we would be doing here is applying the same logic.

It is sometimes argued that corporate executives simply take flight to other countries when taxes are too burdensome, when executive pay is capped, or even when the risk of criminal penalties for white-collar offences is too high. No doubt corporate executives will object to the strengthening of accountability mechanisms on the same basis. Yet we would do well to remember that this priceless pool of talent consists of people who have collectively hastened the end of the species and done nothing to slow down ecocide. This is a pool of talent we would probably be much better off doing without. We now need a different type of structure to replace the existing model of the corporation. And within this structure we will need a different form of management with a different skill set, driven by an entirely different set of motivations and norms.

It is clear that to be effective, any attempt to end the death-grip of the corporation over us will require an end to shareholder primacy and an end to the impunity that is effectively granted to directors and CEOs.

Kill the corporation before it kills us

This book has demonstrated why there is a direct link between the *structure* of the corporation and its limit-less capacity for destruction. We know the problem is one that won't be solved by tinkering around the edges. As Bellamy Foster and his colleagues argue: "if we are to solve our environmental crises, we need to go to the root of the problem: the social relation of capital itself".[48] If the argument developed in this book is even partly correct, this means breaking the organisation that gives material force to the social relations of capital: the corporation.

We need to find the most effective means of ending the corporation's death grip over us. Ultimately, being effective means exploring how we can precipitate a wholesale removal of the rights and privileges of corporate owners and shareholders. Such proposals need to take a strategic approach, one that seeks long-term, permanent change, rather than a short-term tactical, approach.[49] In other words, a strategic approach that requires addressing the material conditions of the social relationships that are abstracted by the corporation. These strategies can only be a starting point in thinking through how regulatory demands and

struggles can undermine the dynamic of capital investment in meaningful ways.

As we have seen, the corporation has played the key
role in facilitating capital's ability to devour nature and
to push past the limits of sustainable development. This
long historical process was predicated on the transformation of public land and goods – held in common –
into private property. The corporation was a key player
in this "theft of the commons". As political theorist
David Ciepley notes, the growth of the corporation was
the crucial dynamic force in this mass transformation
of the form that property took.[50] As we saw in chapter
2 of this book, in the context of colonisation, the corporation has been indispensable in the theft and commodification of people, resources and land. It remains
indispensable for those tasks today. Restoration of the
common ownership of the land and of natural resources
is crucial if we are to reverse climate change. As we
saw in chapters 1 and 2 of this book, the logic of capital accumulation always encourages the devouring of
nature without human and ecological limits. The restoration of common ownership is necessary to remove
the logic of capital accumulation from the stewardship
of the natural environment. Only through a restoration
of the commons can we displace the social dominance
of capital and the corporation over the future of the
planet and allow the damage to our environment to be
repaired.

The corporation is not a problem merely because
it captures natural resources, pollutes and perpetu-

ates a carbon-based economy. As this book has argued, the problem is much more integral to the capitalist system. The corporation eradicates the possibility that we can put the protection of the planet before profit. A fight to get rid of the corporations that have brought us to this point may seem like an impossible task at the moment, but it is necessary for our survival. And it is hardly radical to suggest that if something is killing us, we should over-power it and make it stop. And this is what we need to do. We need to kill the corporation before it kills us.

Notes

PREFACE

1 Hilary Wainwright and Dave Elliot (2016) *The Lucas Plan: A New Trade Unionism in the Making?*, Nottingham: Spokesman.

2 The UK government proudly showcases itself as the second largest defense budget in NATO, with a commitment to expansion, see www.gov.uk/government/publications/international-defence-expenditure-2018/finance-and-economics-annual-statistical-bulletin-international-defence-2018 (accessed 15 May 2020).

3 James Asquith (2020) Grounded flight attendants are being redeployed to hospitals in coronavirus battle, 30 March, *Forbes Magazine*, Available:www.forbes.com/sites/jamesasquith/2020/03/30/grounded-flight-attendants-are-being-redeployed-to-hospitals-in-coronavirus-battle/#676adoc4eb6a (accessed 13 May 2020).

4 Brian Donnelly (2000) Coronavirus: Glasgow BAE Systems workers join battle as 145,000 face shields donated to NHS, *The Herald*, 16 April. Available: www.heraldscotland.com/business_hq/18384973.coronavirus-glasgow-bae-systems-workers-join-battle-145-000-face-shields-donated-nhs-2000-pubs-brewers-offer-takeaway-delivery-chinese-tech-giant-opens-edinburgh/ (accessed 13 May 2020); Bill Jacobs (2020) Coronavirus: BAE's ventilator takes flight from Ribble Valley, *Lancashire Telegraph online*, 2 May. Available: www.lancashiretelegraph.co.uk/news/18422183.coronavirus-baes-ventilator-takes-flight-ribble-valley/ (accessed 13 May 2020).

Notes

5 A copy of the lobbying letter, signed by the European Automobile Manufacturers' Association, the European Association of Automotive Suppliers, the European Tyre & Rubber Manufacturers' Association, and the European Council for Motor Trades and Repairs, is posted here: www.acea.be/uploads/news_documents/COVID19_auto_sector_letter_Von_der_Leyen.pdf (accessed 13 May 2020).

6 Louise Boyle (2020) Oil lobby group asks for environmental laws to be suspended due to coronavirus, *Independent*, 17 April. Available: www.independent.co.uk/environment/oil-lobby-environmental-laws-suspend-canada-climate-change-coronavirus-a9471081.html (accessed 13 May 2020).

7 Jeremy Miller (2020) Trump seizes on pandemic to speed up opening of public lands to industry, *The Guardian*, 30 April. Available: www.theguardian.com/environment/2020/apr/30/public-lands-sale-trump-coronavirus-environmental-regulations (accessed 13 May 2020).

8 Madhur Dhingra et al. (2018) Geographical and Historical Patterns in the Emergences of Novel Highly Pathogenic Avian Influenza (HPAI) H5 and H7 Viruses in Poultry, *Frontiers of Veterinary Science*, vol. 5, no. 84.

9 Grain (2012) *The Great Food Robbery: How Corporations Control Food, Grab Land and Destroy the Climate*, Cape Town: Pambazuka Press.

INTRODUCTION

1 Anna S. Ek, Stefan Löfgren, Johan Bergholm and Ulf Qvarfort (2001) Environmental Effects of One Thousand Years of Copper Production at Falun, Central Sweden, *Ambio*, vol. 30, no. 2: pp. 102–103.

2 Ek et al., Environmental Effects of One Thousand Years of Copper Production, p. 103.

3 Anna S. Ek and Ingemar Renberg (2001) Heavy Metal Pollution and Lake Acidity Changes Caused by One Thousand Years of Copper Mining at Falun, Central Sweden, *Journal of Paleolimnology*, vol. 26, no. 1: pp. 89–107.

4 Stefania Barca (2017) The Labors of Degrowth, *Undisciplined Environments*, 31 January.

5 Ylenia Gostoli (2019) Extinction Rebellion Climate Protests Spread Across UK, *Al Jazeera*, 15 July. Available: www.alja-zeera.com/news/2019/07/extinction-rebellion-climate-pro-tests-spread-uk-190715141008361.html (accessed 5 August 2019).

6 See Polly Higgins, Damien Short and Nigel South (2013) Protecting the Planet: A Proposal for a Law of Ecocide, *Crime, Law and Social Change*, vol. 59, no. 3: pp. 251–266; Damien Short (2016) *Redefining Genocide: Settler Colonialism, Social Death and Ecocide*, London: Zed.

7 Georgia's penal code, for example, specifies a jail term of 8–20 years in length for ecocide. Armenia, Belarus, Moldova and Ukraine have also adopted the offence formally; Anja Gauger, Mai Pouye Rabatel-Fernel, Louise Kulbicki, Damien Short and Polly Higgins (2012) *The Ecocide Project: Ecocide is the missing 5th Crime Against Peace*, London: School of Advanced Study, University of London.

8 The term was coined by scientist Arthur Galston in 1970 who had worked for the US Army in the 1940s and had dis-covered the aggressive herbicide that became Agent Orange. This had first been used in warfare by the British in the bombing of Malay in the 1950s.

9 Richard Falk (1973) Environmental Warfare and Ecocide: Facts, Appraisal, and Proposals, *Bulletin of Peace Proposals*, vol. 4, no. 1: pp. 80–96.

10 Richard Stone (2007) Agent Orange's Bitter Harvest, *Science*, vol. 315, no. 5809, pp. 176–179.

11 Jessica King (2012) U.S. in first effort to clean up Agent Orange in Vietnam, *CNN*, 10 August. Available: https://edition.cnn.com/2012/08/10/world/asia/vietnam-us-agent-orange/ (accessed 5 August 2019).

12 Hisao Furukawa, Mitsuaki Nishibuchi and Yasuyuki Kono (eds.) (2004) *Ecological Destruction, Health, and Development: Advancing Asian Paradigms*, Kyoto and Melbourne: Kyoto University Press and Trans Pacific Press.

13 Monsanto now argues that its predecessor company is an entirely separate enterprise. But this does not stop Agent Orange getting a special mention in the company's offi-

cial history; Monsanto Statement (2017) Agent Orange: Background on Monsanto's Involvement, 7 April. Available: https://monsanto.com/company/media/statements/agent-orange-background/ (accessed 5 August 2019).

14 See US Department of Veteran's Affairs (n.d.) Birth Defects in Children of Women Vietnam Veterans. Available: www.publichealth.va.gov/exposures/agentorange/birth-def ects/children-women-vietnam-vets.asp (accessed 5 August 2019).

15 There are numerous types of organisation that fall into this category: companies that are privately owned by a small number of powerful owners, companies with shares that are bought and sold on "public" stock markets, limited liability partnerships, trusts and so on. The characteristic that unites them is that they are organisations established as independent entities with the primary aim of making a profit for a group of owners, members or shareholders.

16 Jonathan Nitzan and Shimshon Bichler (2009) *Capital as Power: A Study of Order and Creorder*, London: Routledge.

17 Climate Accountability Institute (2019) *Press Release on Carbon Majors Update*, 1965–2017, 9 October.

18 Paul Griffin (2017) *The Carbon Majors Database: CDP Carbon Majors Report 2017*, London: CDP UK.

19 Break Free from Plastic (2018) *Branded: In Search of the World's Top Corporate Plastic Polluters vol. 1*, Washington DC: Greenpeace US.

20 Steve Tombs and David Whyte (2015) *The Corporate Criminal: Why Corporations Must be Abolished*, Abingdon, Oxon; New York: Routledge.

21 See World Health Organization, www.who.int/airpollution/ en/ (accessed 5 August 2019).

22 Michael J. Lynch and Paul Stretesky (2001) Toxic Crimes: Examining Corporate Victimization of the General Public Employing Medical and Epidemiological Evidence, *Critical Criminology*, vol. 10, no. 3: p. 20.

23 Stefania Vitali, James B. Glattfelder and Stefano Battiston (2011) *The Network of Global Corporate Control*, Zurich: Swiss Federal Institute of Technology.

24 Barclays (2019) *Increased Corporate Concentration and the Influence of Market Power*, London: Barclays.

25 United Nations (2015) *The Paris Agreement*, Geneva: United Nations.

26 United Nations (2008) *Kyoto Protocol Reference Manual on Accounting of Emissions and Assigned Amount*, Geneva: United Nations Framework Convention on Climate Change. Available: www.environmental-expert.com/compa nies/keyword-emissions-trading-99, fn. 3, p. 19 (accessed 5 August 2019).

27 In 562 pages of this report, none of those terms are used to problematise the role of corporations, of managers or investors. There are three mentions of "corporations" in chapter 4 of this report. One notes that a small fraction of corporations have adapted to climate change (p. 334), a second notes that multinational corporations have played a role in climate change policy (p. 352) and a third identifies the policy factors inhibiting corporate investment in low carbon economies (p. 378). The word "profit" is used 4 times. First, in the political sense rather than in the context of monetary profit (p. 79, chapter 1) and in the other 3 uses, to make the claim that reducing carbon emissions is likely to be profitable (pp. 341, 365, 386 and 486). The word "company" appears twice in passive usage in the glossary at the end of the report. The word manager is only used 3 times, all in the context of specialist managers (ethical investment (p. 374), "resource" (p. 485) and forestry managers (p. 509), rather than in the sense of corporate management generally); Intergovernmental Panel on Climate Change (2018) *Special Report on Global Warming of 1.5°*, Geneva: United Nations.

28 World Bank Group (2016) *Climate Change Action Plan 2016–2020*, Washington, International Bank for Reconstruction and Development/The World Bank. The words "company" and "corporation" are only used to refer to a very small number of "good practice" investors and international finance corporations. The words "shareholder" and "director" are only used to refer to the Word Bank's own shareholders and directors.

29 Climate and Clean Air Coalition and World Health Organization (2015) *Reducing Global Health Risks Through Mitigation of Short-Lived Climate Pollutants: Scoping Report for Policymakers*, Geneva: World Health Organisation.

30 A.J. Cohen, J. M. Samet, K. Straif and International Agency for Research on Cancer (2013) *Air Pollution and Cancer*, Lyon: International Agency for Research on Cancer. The only mention of the word "company" in this report is in reference to sponsors.

31 Alexandria Ocasio-Cortez (2019) Recognizing the Duty of the Federal Government to Create a Green New Deal, 116th Congress, 1st Session, House of Representatives. Available: https://ocasio-cortez.house.gov/sites/ocasio-cortez.house. gov/files/Resolution%20on%20a%20Green%20New% 20Deal.pdf (accessed 5 August 2019).

32 Stefania Barca (2016) Labor in the age of climate Change, *Jacobin*, 18 March. Available: www.jacobinmag.com/ 2016/03/climate-labor-just-transition-green-jobs/ (accessed 5 August 2019).

33 For example, new forms of chronic kidney disease; see Ciara Kierans (2019) *Chronic Failures: Kidneys, Regimes of Care and the Mexican State*, New Brunswick: Rutgers University Press.

34 Desmond Tutu (2019) The Threat of Climate Change is the Apartheid of Our Times, *Financial Times*, 4 October.

35 Naomi Oreskes and Erik M. Conway (2010) *Merchants of Doubt: How a Handful of Scientists Obscured the Truth on Issues from Tobacco Smoke to Global Warming*, London: Bloomsbury; L.A. Bero (2005); Tobacco Industry Manipulation of Research, *Public Health Reports*, vol. 120: p. 9; Brendan Montague, How the neoliberal dream became the reality of Thatcherism, *The Ecologist*, 9 August.

36 Geoffrey Tweedale (2001) *Magic Mineral to Killer Dust: Turner & Newall and the Asbestos Hazard*, Oxford: Oxford University Press.

37 A summary of precisely the same process of corporate denial and distortion surrounding the fatal nature of their products can be found in food production and sales, in

pharmaceuticals, in agricultural products, in textile and clothing production, in electronics production and on and on and on. David Naguib Pellow (2000) *Resisting Global Toxins*, Cambridge, MA: MIT Press; John Stauber and Sheldon Rampton (1995) *Toxic Sludge is Good for You*, New York: Common Courage; David Michaels (2008) *Doubt is Their Product*, Oxford: Oxford University Press; Evaline Lubbers (ed.) (2002) *Battling Big Business: Countering Greenwash, Infiltration and Other Forms of Corporate Bullying*, Dartington, Devon: Green.

38 Massachusetts Institute of Technology News Office (2017) *Study: Volkswagen's excess emissions will lead to 1,200 premature deaths in Europe*, Press Release, 3 March. Available: http://news.mit.edu/2017/volkswagen-emissions-prematu re-deaths-europe-0303 (accessed 5 August 2019).

39 It regularly won CSR awards, including the World Forum for Ethics in Business for responsible action in the environmental and social fields, 2014. For a full list of its 2014 awards, see the Volkswagen Group Annual Report for 2014/15. Available: https://annualreport2014.volkswagenag.com/group-management-report/sustainable-value-enhancement/environmental-management/environmental-awards.html (accessed 5 August 2019).

40 Jack Ewing (2018) 10 Monkeys and a Beetle: Inside VW's Campaign for "Clean Diesel", *New York Times*, 25 January.

41 Patrick McGee (2018) Car Emissions Scandal: Loopholes in the Lab Tests, *Financial Times*, 7 August.

42 Kadhim Shubber (2019) Fiat Chrysler Agrees to Pay $800m to Settle Emissions Cheating Case, *Financial Times*, 10 January.

43 BBC News (2018) Nissan admits falsifying emissions tests in Japan, 9 July. Available: www.bbc.co.uk/news/business-44763905 (accessed 5 August 2019).

44 BBC News (2016) Renault to modify 15,000 new cars in emission scare, 19 January. Available: www.bbc.co.uk/news/business-35350474 (accessed 5 August 2019).

45 BBC News (2018) Daimler forced to recall Mercedes with defeat devices, 11 June. Available: www.bbc.co.uk/news/business-44444361 (accessed 5 August 2019).

46 Kentaro Iwoamoto (2016) Mitsubishi Motors rigged fuel economy tests for more than 600,000 cars. Nikkei Asian Review, 20 April. Available: https://asia.nikkei.com/Business/Companies/Mitsubishi-Motors-rigged-fuel-econ omy-tests-for-more-than-600-000-cars (accessed 5 August 2019).

47 Indeed an update of Ralph Nader's classic book on corporate crime in the industry, *Unsafe at Any Speed: The Designed-In Dangers of the American Automobile* (1965, Chicago: Grossman) is long overdue.

48 See, for example, W. Shaw (2011) *Business Ethics: A Textbook With Cases*, 7th ed., Boston, MA: Wadsworth; and D. Birsch and J. Fielder (1994) *The Ford Pinto Case: A Study in Applied Ethics*, New York: State University of New York Press. Ford had calculated that if there were 180 burn deaths and 180 serious injuries per year, the social cost of this (and the cost to Ford) would be much less than the $11 cost per vehicle needed to modify the fuel system to make it safer and avoid the deaths. The car was marketed without modification, largely on the basis of this calculation. It is unknown how many people died as a consequence, but it was almost certainly more than Ford's "tolerable" figure of 180 deaths.

49 David Whyte (2016) It's Common Sense, Stupid! Corporate Crime and Techniques of Neutralization in the Automobile Industry, *Crime, Law and Social Change*, vol. 66, no. 2, pp. 165–181.

50 *New York Times*, 1 November, 2017; *Financial Times*, 3 May 2019.

51 Neela Banerjee, Lisa Song and David Hasemyer (2015) Exxon's Own Research Confirmed Fossil Fuels' Role in Global Warming Decades Ago, *Inside Climate News*, 16 September. Available: https://insideclimatenews.org/news/15092015/Exxons-own-research-confirmed-fossil-fuels-role-in-global-warming (accessed 5 August 2019).

52 Exxon Research and Engineering Company, internal memo, dated 5 February 1981: p. 2. Available: http://insidecli matenews.org/sites/default/files/documents/Exxon%20Re view%20of%20Climate%20Research%20Program%20%281981%29.pdf (accessed 5 August 2019).

53 Koch Family Foundations is a charitable trust funded by Koch Industries, the US oil, gas, paper and chemical conglomerate, which is currently the second-largest privately owned company in the US.

54 Justin Farrell (2016) Corporate Funding and Ideological Polarization about Climate Change, *Proceedings of the National Academy of Sciences of the United States of America*, vol. 113, no. 1: pp. 92–97.

55 Eveline Lubbers (2012) *Secret Manoeuvres in the Dark: Corporate and Police Spying on Activists*, London: Pluto Press.

56 J. Maxwell and F. Briscoe (1997) There's Money in the Air: The CFC ban and DuPont's Regulatory Strategy, *Business Strategy and the Environment*, vol. 6, no. 5, pp. 276–286.

57 Michael Weisskopf (1988) CFCs: Rise and Fall of Chemical "Miracle", *The Washington Post*, 10 April.

58 James Lovelock (2019) *Novascene: The Coming of Age of Hyperintelligence*, London: Allen Lane: p. 38.

59 Herbert L. Needleman (1998) Clair Patterson and Robert Kehoe: Two Views on Lead Toxicity, *Environmental Research*, vol. 78, no. 2: pp. 79–85.

60 Beth Gardiner (2019) *Choked: The Age of Air Pollution and the Fight for a Cleaner Future*, London: Granta.

61 Sarah A. Vogel (2009) The Politics of Plastics: The Making and Unmaking of Bisphenol, *American Journal of Public Health*, vol. 99 (Suppl 3): S559–S566.

62 Mariah Blake (2014) The Scary New Evidence on BPA-Free Plastics and the Big Tobacco-Style Campaign to Bury it, *Mother Jones*, March/April.

63 Market Watch (2019) *Bisphenol A (BPA) market 2019 global leading players, industry updates, future growth, business prospects, forthcoming developments and future investments by forecast to 2025*, Press Release, 19 March. Available: www.marketwatch.com/press-release/bisphenol-a-bpa-market-2019-global-leading-players-industry-updates-future-growth-business-prospects-forthcoming-developments-and-future-investments-by-forecast-to-2025-2019-03-19 (accessed 5 August 2019).

64 G. Markowitz and D. Rosner (2018) Monsanto, PCBs, and

the Creation of a "World-Wide Ecological Problem", *Journal of Public Health Policy*, vol. 39, no. 4: pp. 463–540.

65 See the archive established by the Bioscience Resource Project and the Center for Media and Democracy. Available: www.poisonpapers.org/the-poison-papers/ (accessed 5 August 2019).

66 Cited in Marie-Monique Robin (2014) *Our Daily Poison: From Pesticides to Packaging, How Chemicals Have Contaminated the Food Chain and Are Making us Sick*, New York: The New Press: p. 195.

67 Jim Morris (1998) In Strictest Confidence: The Chemical Industry's Secrets, *Houston Chronicle*. Part One: Toxic Secrecy, 28 June, pp. 1A, 24A–27A; Part Two: High-Level Crime, 29 June, pp. 1A, 8A, 9A; and Part Three: Bane on the Bayou, 26 July, pp. 1A, 16A; Bill Moyers, Trade Secrets: A Moyers Report, aired 26 March 2001, on the US network Public Broadcasting Service.

68 Erika L. Robb and Mari B. Baker (2018) *Organophosphate Toxicity*. StatPearls, National Center for Biotechnology Information.

69 Susie Neilson (2018) The Pesticide Industry Has Wanted to Gut Endangered Species' Protections: Under Trump, It's Happening, *Mother Jones*, 26 July. Available: www.mother jones.com/environment/2018/07/thanks-to-trump-pesti cide-companies-are-now-free-to-kill-all-the-endangered-spe cies-they-want/ (accessed 5 August 2019).

70 Market Insider (2017) *Global organophosphate market worth $10.33 Billion by 2025*, Press Release, 7 November. Available: https://markets.businessinsider.com/news/stoc ks/global-organophosphate-market-worth-10-33-billion-by-2025-cagr-4-8-global-market-estimates-1007206631 (accessed 5 August 2019).

71 Nathan Donley and Carey Gillam (2019) The EPA is Meant to Protect Us: The Monsanto Trials Suggest it Isn't Doing That, *Guardian*, 7 May. Available: www.theguardian.com/commentisfree/2019/may/07/epa-monsanto-round-up-trial (accessed 5 August 2019).

72 Strictly speaking, it is the by-products of PVC that are highly persistent and bio-accumulative. BPA and glyphosate

are strictly defined as non-persistent chemical compounds. However, this strict definition can be misleading, partly because of the way evidence is used and partly because of the way definitions are framed. Because BPA has been shown to alter the reproductive system of animals this means it is chronically present in our environment and therefore functions as a persistent chemical. Recent studies of the half-life of glyphosate in water and soil found it to be much more persistent than previously thought; John Peterson Myers et al. (2016) Concerns Over Use of Glyphosate-Based Herbicides and Risks Associated with Exposures: A Consensus Statement, *Environmental Health*. vol. 15 (article number 19).

CHAPTER 1

1 Paul Johnson (2010) *Making the Market: The Victorian Origins of Corporate Capitalism*, Cambridge: Cambridge University Press.
2 Rebecca Spencer (2004) *Corporate Law and Structures: Exposing the Roots of the Problem*, Oxford: Corporate Watch.
3 Claudia I. Janssen (2013) Corporate Historical Responsibility (CHR): Addressing a Corporate Past of Forced Labor at Volkswagen, *Journal of Applied Communication Research*, vol. 41, no. 1: pp. 64–83.
4 Peter Hayes (2001) *Industry and Ideology: IG Farben in the Nazi Era*, Cambridge: Cambridge University Press.
5 See the report by Greenpeace East Asia. Available: www.greenpeace.org/eastasia/news/stories/toxics/2009/BASF-factory-China/ (accessed 5 August 2019).
6 Matthias Blamont (2018) Sanofi Halts Production at Pyrenees Plant After Pollution Complaint, *Reuters*, 9 July.
7 See the US Environmental Protection Agency documents. Available: www.epa.gov/hwcorrectiveactionsites/hazardo us-waste-cleanup-agfa-corporation-peerless-photo-products-shoreham (accessed 5 August, 2019).
8 Political Economy Research Institute (2016) Toxic 100 Air Polluters Index. Available: www.peri.umass.edu/toxic-100-

air-polluters-index-2016-report-based-on-2014-data (accessed 5 August 2019).

9   Tina Bellon (2018.) Bayer CEO Says Would Consider Glyphosate Settlement Depending on Costs, *Reuters*, 2 November.

10 Amigos da Terra Brasil and Amigos de la Tierra Uruguay (n.d.) *What You Should Know About Stora Enso Fact Sheet: South America*. Available: www.foei.org/wp-content/up loads/2014/01/Fact-Sheet-Stora-Enso-2010.pdf (accessed 5 August 2019).

11 Zygmunt Bauman (1989) *Modernity and the Holocaust*, Oxford: Polity Press.

12 Sir George Mackenzie (1678) *The laws and customes of Scotland, in matters criminal wherein is to be seen how the civil law, and the laws and customs of other nations do agree with, and supply ours*, Edinburgh: James Glen.

13 David Millon (1990) Theories of the Corporation, *Duke Law Journal*, vol. 39, no. 2: pp. 201–262.

14 As early as 1809, the US courts (Bank of US v Deveaux 1809) were asked to rule on whether or not corporations could be regarded as "citizens" for the purposes of their ability to sue other, flesh and blood, citizens. In a number of cases the courts went back and forwards on this question, before settling on the formulation in 1844 that: a "corporation received the jurisdictional opportunities open to citizens without the Court having to accord 'citizenship' to it" (Louisville, C. & C.R. Co. v Letson 1844). This judgement pretty much represents the situation today: corporations are "citizens" for some legal purposes, if not regarded as such in the broadest constitutional sense; J. Krannich (2005) The Corporate "Person": A New Analytical Approach to a Flawed Method of Constitutional Interpretation, *Loyola University Chicago Law Journal*, vol. 37, no. 1: pp. 61–109. Available: https://lawecommons.luc.edu/cgi/viewcontent. cgi?article=1200&context=luclj (accessed 5 August 2019).

15 For different perspectives that reach the same conclusion, see Morton J. Horwitz (1985) Santa Clara Revisited: The Development of Corporate Theory, *West Virginia Law Review*, vol. 88: pp. 173–224; Melvin A. Eisenberg (1999) The

Conception That the Corporation is a Nexus of Contracts, and the Dual Nature of the Firm, *Journal of Corporate Law*, vol. 24: pp. 819–836; and Larry E. Ribstein (2010) *The Rise of the Uncorporation*, New York: Oxford University Press.

16 Ronald. H. Coase (1953) The Nature of the Firm, in Kenneth E. Boulding and George J. Stigler (eds.) *Readings in Price Theory*, London: George Allen and Unwin. See also Michael C. Jensen and William H. Meckling (1976) The Theory of the Firm: Managerial Behaviour, Agency Costs, and Ownership Structure, *Journal of Financial Economics*, vol. 3, no. 4: pp. 305–360.

17 *Santa Clara County v. Southern Pacific Railroad Company*, 118 U.S. 394 (1886).

18 Stefanie Khoury and David Whyte (2017) *Corporate Human Rights Violations: Global Prospects for Legal Action*, Abingdon: Routledge.

19 Harry Glasbeek (2012) Contortions of Corporate Law: James Hardie Reveals Cracks in Liberal Law's Armour, *Australian Journal of Corporate Law*, vol. 27: pp. 132–168.

20 *Citizens United v. Federal Election Commission*, 558 U.S. 310 (2010).

21 Council of Europe (1985) *Collected Edition of the Travaux Préparatoires of the European Convention on Human Rights*, Vol. VII. Leiden: Martinus Nijhoff ECHR

22 Marcus Emberland (2006) *The Human Rights of Companies: Exploring the Structure of ECHR Protection*, Oxford: Oxford UniversityPress.

23 Khoury and Whyte, *Corporate Human Rights Violations*.

24 Sarah Anderson and Manuel Pérez Rocha (2013) *Mining for Profits in International Tribunals: Lessons for the Trans-Pacific Partnership*, Washington DC: Institute for Policy Studies.

25 Naomi Klein (2014) *This Changes Everything*, London: Penguin

26 Jared Bernstein and Lori Wallach (2016) The New Rules of the Road: A Progressive Approach to Globalization, *American Prospect*. Available: https://prospect.org/article/new-rules-road-progressive-approach-globalization (accessed 5 August 2019).

27 Michael Parenti (2011) *The Face of Imperialism*, Abingdon: Routledge.

28 Pablo Ciocchini and Stefanie Khoury (2018) Investor State Dispute Settlement: Institutionalising "Corporate Exceptionality", *Oñati Socio-legal Series*, vol. 8, no. 6: pp. 976–1000.

29 Kerry Kennedy (2019) Chevron and Cultural Genocide in Ecuador, *Common Dreams*, 14 December. Available: www.commondreams.org/views/2009/12/14/chevron-and-cultural-genocide-ecuador (accessed 5 August 2019).

30 S. Totten, W. Parsons and R. Hitchcock (2002) Confronting Genocide and Ethnocide of Indigenous Peoples, in A. Hinton (ed.) *Anihillating Difference: The Anthropology of Genocide*, Berkley: University of California Press; Debra Abelowitz (2001) Discrimination and Cultural Genocide in the Oil Fields of Ecuador: The U.S. as a Forum for International Dispute, *New England International and Comparative Law Annual*, vol. 7: pp. 145–153; see the report at Amazon Watch (n.d.). Available: https://amazonwatch.org/work/chevron (accessed 5 August 2019).

31 *La República*, 26 November 2014. Available: https://larepublica.pe/politica/836972-fiscalia-acusa-a-petrolera-por-intento-de-genocidio/ (accessed 5 August 2019).

32 Khoury and Whyte, *Corporate Human Rights Violations*; Peter Muchlinski (2001) Human Rights and Multinationals: Is There a Problem? *International Affairs*, vol. 77, no. 1: pp. 31–47.

33 William Holden, Kathleen Nadeau and Dan Jacobson (2011) Exemplifying Accumulation by Dispossession: Mining and Indigenous Peoples in the Philippines, *Geografiska Annaler*, vol. 93, no. 2: pp. 141–161; Tom Perreault (2012) Dispossession by Accumulation? Mining, Water and the Nature of Enclosure on the Bolivian Altiplano, *Antipode*, vol. 45: pp. 1050–1069.

34 Phillipe Le Billion (2012) *Wars of Plunder: Conflicts, Profits and the Politics of Resources*, London: Hurst and Company.

35 Grietje Baars (2017) Capital, Corporate Citizenship and Legitimacy, in Grietje Baars and André Spicer (eds.) *The*

Corporation: A Critical, Multi-Disciplinary Handbook, Cambridge: Cambridge University Press.

36 In 2017, New Zealand granted the status of legal personhood to the Whanganui River, the third longest in the country. There is a growing movement that demands personhood status for natural resources – rivers and lakes – as a means of protection that allows contracted and constitutional "rights". Report available: https://e360.yale.edu/features/should-rivers-have-rights-a-growing-movement-says-its-about-time, 12 August 2018 (accessed 5 August 2019).

37 M. Anderson (2001) Transnational Corporations and Environmental Damage: Is Tort Law the Answer?, *Washburn Law Journal,* vol. 41, no. 3: pp. 399–426; Khoury and Whyte, *Corporate Human Rights Violations,* pp. 77–78.

38 Frank Pearce and Steve Tombs (2012) *Bhopal: Flowers at the Altar of Profit and Power,* North Somercotes: CrimeTalk Books.

39 See the statement on Dow's website: https://corporate.dow.com/en-us/about/issues-and-challenges/bhopal/tragedy.

40 Pearce and Tombs, *Bhopal: Flowers at the Altar of Profit and Power.*

41 The quid-pro-quo for the advantages of limited liability is that shareholders become "residual claimants" on the company's revenue or assets. All other parties in law have a fixed return from the corporation (workers in agreed wages, creditors in agreed debts and interest payments etc). The shareholder is only entitled to a variable combination of income (left over after other costs are payed) and the value of the share, which is also variable.

42 Charles Ferguson (2012) *Inside Job: The Financiers Who Pulled off the Heist of the Century,* London: Oneworld.

43 David Friedrichs (2011) Occupy Wall Street Does Have a Clear Message, *Marketwatch,* 24 October. Available: www.marketwatch.com/story/occupy-wall-street-does-have-a-clear-message-2011-10-24 (accessed 5 August 2019).

44 Gregg Barak (2012) *Theft of a Nation: Wall Street Looting and Federal Regulatory Colluding,* Lanham, MD: Rowman and Littlefield: p. 95.

45 The only criminal case against a bank chief executive for

charges related to the financial crisis began in June 2017, when the Serious Fraud Office announced charges against four former Barclays executives. At the time of writing, the case is ongoing; J. Croft, and B. Thompson (2017) Former Barclays Executives in Dock to Face Criminal Charges, *Financial Times*, 3 July.

46 Victoria Fincle (2016) The Big Fish Seen Escaping an Agency Pursuing Bank Fraud, *New York Times*, 28 July.

47 The 10 largest total penalties imposed by the US Government on financial institutions, in billions, are as follows: Bank of America ($76.1); JPMorgan Chase ($43.7); Citigroup ($19); Deutsche Bank ($14); Wells Fargo ($11.8); RBS ($10.1); BNP Paribas ($9.3); Credit Suisse ($9.1); Morgan Stanley ($8.6); Goldman Sachs ($7.7); and UBS ($6.5); Steve Goldstein (2018), Here's The Staggering Amount Banks Have Been Fined Since the Financial Crisis, *Marketwatch*, 24 February. Available: www.marketwatch.com/story/banks-have-been-fined-a-staggering-243-billion-since-the-financial-crisis-2018-02-20 (accessed 5 August 2019).

48 Steve Tombs and David Whyte (2007) *Safety Crimes*, Collumpton: Willan.

49 David Whyte (2010) An Intoxicated Politics of Regulation, in Hannah Quirk, Toby Seddon and Graham Smith (eds.) *Regulation and Criminal Justice: Innovations in Policy and Research*, Cambridge: Cambridge University Press.

50 *The New York Times*, 14 July 1912.

51 Roger Casement (1997) *The Amazon Journal of Roger Casement* (ed. A Mitchell), Dublin: Lilyput: p. 504.

52 *The Economist*, 20 July 1912.

53 L.L. Lan and L. Heracleous (2010) Rethinking Agency Theory: The View From Law, *Academy of Management Review*, vol. 35, no. 2: p. 22.

54 Otto Gierke (1900) *Political Theories of the Middle Age* (trans. F.W. Maitland), Cambridge: Cambridge University Press.

55 This perspective is also known as pluralism; Philip J. Stern (2017) The Corporation in History, in Grietje Baars and Andre Spicer (eds.) *The Corporation: A Critical, Multi-Disciplinary Handbook*, Cambridge: Cambridge University Press. For useful reviews of this perspective, see

M. Hagar (1989) Bodies Politic: The Progressive History of Organizational Real Entity Theory, *University of Pittsburg Law Review*, vol. 50: pp. 575–654; and Millon, Theories of the Corporation.

56 Harold Laski (1916) The Personality of Associations, *Harvard Law Review*, vol. 29, no. 4: p 405.

57 E. Merrick Dodd Jr. (1932) For Whom are Corporate Managers Trustees, *Harvard Law Review*, vol. 45, no. 7: pp. 1160; emphasis added.

58 *Dodge v. Ford Motor Company*, 204 Mich. 459, 170 N.W. 668 (Mich. 1919)

59 A. Gamble and G. Kelly (2001) Shareholder Value and the Stakeholder Debate in the UK, *Corporate Governance*, vol. 9, no. 2: pp. 110–117.

60 Paddy Ireland (1999) Company Law and the Myth of Shareholder Ownership, *Modern Law Review*, vol. 62, no. 1: pp. 32–57.

61 Michel Aglietta and Antoine Rebérioux (2005) *Corporate Governance Adrift: A Critique of Shareholder Value*, Cheltenham: Edward Elgar.

62 The financial responsibility imposed on directors by law is known as a "fiduciary duty".

63 John Parkinson (1993) *Corporate Power and Responsibility*, Oxford: Oxford University Press: p. 77.

64 Adolph Berle (1964) *The 20th Century Capitalist Revolution*, New York: Harcourt, Brace and World; Adolph Berle and Gardiner C. Means (1991) *The Modern Corporation and Private Property*, New Brunswick: Transaction.

65 Berle and Means, *The Modern Corporation and Private Property*: p. 312. Although they opened up arguments for new forms of accountability, the conclusions drawn by Berle and Means fell back on the reasoning that had been established in *Dodge vs Ford*. In doing so, their analysis created a clear separation between the goals of investors (a relatively fast profit) and the goals of managers (career success, stable income and wealth).

66 Frank Pearce (1993) Corporate Rationality as Corporate Crime, *Studies in Political Economy*, vol. 40, no. 1: p. 135–162.

67 Henry W. Ballantine (1925) Separate Entity of Parent and Subsidiary Corporations, *California Law Review*, vol. 14, no. 1: pp. 12–21.

68 Gerald A. Epstein. (2005) Introduction: Financialisation and the World Economy, in Gerald A. Epstein (ed.), *Financialisation and the World Economy*, Cheltenham: Edward Elgar.

69 Paddy Ireland (2007) Capitalism Without the Capitalist: The Joint Stock Company Share and the Emergence of the Modern Doctrine of Separate Corporate Personality, *Journal of Legal History*, vol. 17, no. 1: p. 45.

70 Paddy Ireland, Ian Grigg-Spall and Dave Kelly (1987) The Conceptual Foundations of Modern Company Law, *Journal of Law and Society*, vol 14, no. 1: p. 162.

71 Ireland, Capitalism Without the Capitalist.

72 T. Macalister (2010) Shell Faces Shareholder Revolt over Canadian Tar Sands Project, *Guardian*, 18 January; S. Williams (2010) Power Struggle Over Canada's "Dirty Oil" Sands, *The Telegraph*, 6 May.

73 Susanne Soederberg (2010) *Corporate Power and Ownership in Contemporary Capitalism: The Politics of Resistance and Domination*, London: Routledge.

74 The Company Law Review Steering Group (2001) *Modern Company Law for a Competitive Economy: The Final Report, Vol. 1*, London: UK Government Department of Trade and Industry.

75 Casement, *The Amazon Journal of Roger Casement*; House of Commons Trade and Industry Committee (2003) *The White Paper on Modernising Company Law Sixth Report of Session 2002–03*, London: The Stationery Office.

76 A rentier is a person whose main source of income is from someone whose income derives from rents, interest, or returns on investments. On the fundamental purpose of the corporation, see Harry Glasbeek (2002) *Wealth By Stealth: Corporate Crime, Corporate Law and the Perversion of Democracy*, Toronto: Between the Lines; Maurice Zeitlin (1974) Corporate Ownership and Control: The Large Corporation and the Capitalist Class, *American Journal of Sociology*, vol. 79, no. 5: pp. 1073–1119; Ireland, Company

Law and the Myth of Shareholder Ownership; Frank Pearce and Steve Tombs (1998) *Toxic Capitalism: Corporate Crime in the Chemical Industry*, Aldershot: Ashgate.

Chapter 2

1 World Rainforest Movement (2018). Finnish Activists Protest Against Stora Enso and Veracel, *WRM Bulletin*, vol. 237. Available: https://wrm.org.uy/other-relevant-informati on/finnish-activists-protest-against-stora-enso-and-veracel/ (accessed 5 August 2019).
2 Markus Kröger (2010) The Politics of Pulp Investment and the Brazilian Landless Movement (MST) *Acta Politica*, No 39, Helsinki: University of Helsinki.
3 FSC-Watch (n.d.) Military Police Violently Evict Women Protesters From Stora Enso's Plantations in Brazil. Available: https://fsc-watch.com/2008/03/07/military-pol ice-violently-evict-women-protesters-from-stora-ensos-plan tations-in-brazil/ (accessed 5 August 2019).
4 Chris Lang (2008) *Plantations, Poverty and Power*, Swedish Society for Nature Conservation, Oxfam Netherlands and World Rainforest Movement.
5 Statement 24 April 2012 to the Stora Enso Annual General Meeting, Helsinki. Available: https://maattomienliike.word press.com/2012/04/25/stora-enso-rethink-now/ (accessed 5 August 2019).
6 Stora Enso (2018) *Annual Report*, Helsinki: Stora Enso: p. 13.
7 A transnational corporation operates in more than one country, normally with a dispersed organisational and ownership structure that allows it to have different management hierarchies and headquarters in the various countries it operates in.
8 Ellen Meiksins Wood (2000) Capitalism or Enlightenment, *History of Political Thought*, vol. 21, no. 3: pp. 405–426.
9 M. Freeman, R. Pearson and J. Taylor (2013) Law, Politics and the Governance of English and Scottish Joint-Stock Companies, 1600–1850, *Business History*, vol. 55, no. 4: pp. 636–652.

10 George Robb (1992) *White Collar Crime in Modern England: Financial Fraud and Business Morality 1845–1929*, Cambridge: Cambridge University Press.

11 Oliver Bullough (2018) *Moneyland: Why Thieves And Crooks Now Rule The World And How To Take It Back*, London: Profile: p. 91.

12 Robb, *White Collar Crime in Modern England*.

13 David Wallace-Wells (2019) *The Uninhabitable Earth: A Story of the Future*, London: Penguin.

14 A review of the data on the growth of trade indicates that the first wave of globalisation began in the early 1800s; Bank of International Settlements (2017) *87th Annual Report*, Basle: BIS.

15 R. Nelson (1959) *Merger Movements in American Industry 1895–1956*, Princeton: Princeton University Press.

16 Between 1500 and 1800, global trade grew around 1% on average per annum. In 1820, it was 3.5%, and by 1870 had begun to grow exponentially.

17 Karl Marx (1973) *Grundrisse: Introduction to the Critique of Political Economy*, Harmondsworth: Penguin: p. 524.

18 Geographer David Harvey put it slightly differently, as "time-space compression"; David Harvey (1989) *The Condition of Postmodernity*, Oxford: Blackwell.

19 For example, J.D. Ward, P.C. Sutton, A.D. Werner, R. Costanza, S.H. Mohr and C.T. Simmons (2016) Is Decoupling GDP Growth from Environmental Impact Possible? *PLoS ONE*, vol. 11, no. 3: pp. 1–14.

20 John Bellamy Foster (2009) The Absolute General Law of Environmental Degradation Under Capitalism, *Capitalism Nature Socialism*, vol. 3, no. 3: p. 79.

21 John Bellamy Foster (2008) Marx's Grundrisse and the Ecological Contradictions of Capitalism, in Marcello Musto (ed.) *Karl Marx's Grundrisse: Foundations of the Critique of Political Economy 150 Years Later*, London: Routledge: p. 101.

22 James O'Connor (1988) Capitalism Nature Socialism: A Theoretical Introduction, *Capitalism Nature Socialism*, vol. 1, no. 1: pp. 11–38.

23 John Bellamy Foster, Brett Clark and Richard York (2010)

The Ecological Rift: Capitalism's War on the Earth, New York: Monthly Review Press.

24 Bellamy Foster, Clark and York, *The Ecological Rift*: p. 59.

25 Charles Ffoulkes (1937) *The Gun-Founders of England: With a List of English and Continental Gun-Founders from the XIV to the XIX Centuries*, Cambridge: Cambridge University Press: p. 32.

26 Frank B. Cross and Robert A. Prentice (2007) *Law and Corporate Finance*, Cheltenham: Edward Elgar.

27 Robert Knox (2016) Valuing Race? Stretched Marxism and the Logic of Imperialism, *London Review of International Law*, vol. 4, no. 1: p. 126.

28 W. Pencak (2011) *Historical Dictionary of Colonial America*, Lanham, Maryland: Rowman and Littlefield.

29 H.L. Osgood (1896) The Corporation as a Form of Colonial Government, *Political Science Quarterly*, vol. 11, no. 2: p. 259.

30 Adam Winkler (2018) *We the Corporations: How American Businesses Won Their Civil Rights*, New York: Liveright.

31 Eric Williams (1944) *Capitalism and Slavery*, Richmond, Virginia: University of North Carolina Press.

32 Williams, *Capitalism and Slavery*.

33 The English East India Company became the British East India Company following the Treaty of Union in 1707 that united the English and Scottish crowns.

34 Karl Marx (1857) The Indian Revolt, *New-York Daily Tribune*, 16 September.

35 Philip Lawson (1993) *The East India Company: A History, 1600–1857*, London: Routledge.

36 Nick Robins (2006) *The Corporation that Changed the World: How the East India Company Shaped the Modern Multinational*, London: Pluto: p. 27.

37 For example, the Company of Royal Adventurers Trading to Africa, the earlier name of the Royal African Company, was established partly with the private funds of King Charles II and his brother James, Duke of York, who led the company and then later took the throne as James II; both companies enjoyed royal patronage and personal investment by members of the Royal family. Although the Royal family had no

direct interest in the East India Company when it was established, its Court of Directors was, throughout its history, peppered with nobility and significant politicians.

38 Utsa Patnaik (2018) Revisiting the Drain, or Transfer from India to Britain in the Context of Global Diffusion of Capitalism, in Shubhra Chakrabarti and Utsa Patnaik (eds.) *Agrarian and Other Histories: Essays for Binay Bhushan*, New York: Colombia University Press.

39 Winkler, *We the Corporations*.

40 This is a different account to that offered by Ellen Meiksins Wood, who argues that in so far as those colonial corporations operated primarily to harness trade, rather than expand productive capacities, they were quintessentially non-capitalist organisations, Ellen Meiksins Wood (2003) *Empire of Capital*, London: Verso.

41 Shubhra Chakrabarti (2018) Introduction, in Shubhra Chakrabarti and Utsa Patnaik (eds.) *Agrarian and Other Histories: Essays for Binay Bhushan*, New York: Colombia University Press.

42 John Bellamy Foster and Robert W. McChesney (2011) The Internet's Unholy Marriage to Capitalism, *Monthly Review*, vol. 62, no. 10: pp. 1–30.

43 Bellamy Foster, Clark and York, *The Ecological Rift*: p. 370; Lucia Pradella (2017) Marx and the Global South: Connecting History and Value Theory, *Sociology*, vol. 51, no. 1: pp. 146–161.

44 Adam Hochschild (2016) *Spain in Our Hearts: Americans in the Spanish Civil War, 1936–1939*, London: Macmillan; Reiber was known to be a supporter of the German Third Reich. Texaco continued to ship oil into Germany during World War II and Reiber embarked on a tour of German factories with Herman Goering in 1939.

45 This point is officially recognised by the Spanish government; *Guardian*, 13 July 2018.

46 Hochschild, *Spain in Our Hearts*.

47 Daniel Guerin (1973) *Fascism and Big Business*, New York: Pathfinder.

48 A. Sutton (1976) *Wall Street and the Rise of Hitler*, New Rochelle, New York: Arlington House Publishers.

49 BBC Online (1998) Europe Swiss Banks Dodge Sanctions in Holocaust Deal, Friday 21 August. Available: http://news.bbc.co.uk/1/hi/world/europe/70515.stm (accessed 5 August 2019).

50 Antony Barnett (1999) Holocaust Shame of Barclays, *Guardian*, 28 March.

51 Paul Beckett (2000) Chase Manhattan Bank Uncovers Deal That Aided Nazi Germany, *The Wall Street Journal*, 23 February.

52 Michael Dobbs (1998) Ford and GM Scrutinized for Alleged Nazi Collaboration, *Washington Post*, 30 November.

53 Anthony Sampson (1973) *The Sovereign State of ITT*, London: Coronet.

54 M. Mintz and J. Cohen (1977) *Power, Inc.: Public and Private Rulers and How to Make Them Accountable*, New York: Bantam Books.

55 Edwin Black (2001) *IBM and the Holocaust: The Strategic Alliance Between Nazi Germany and America's Most Powerful Corporation*, London: Little, Brown; and Edwin Black (2009) *Nazi Nexus: America's Corporate Connections to Hitler's Holocaust*, Washington, DC: Dialog Press.

56 Martin Bailey (1979) *Oilgate: The Sanctions Scandal*, London: Coronet.

57 Corporations like Dole have been implicated in the use of military and paramilitaries to intimidate trade unionists (in Philippines, see: www.ituc-csi.org/IMG/pdf/new_final_philippines_tpr_2012.pdf; accessed 5 August 2019) and Del Monte (in Guatemala, see "Protest re killing in Guatemala", Letter 14 February 2012 From Brendan Barber, TUC General Secretary to H.E. Mr Acisclo Valladares Molina, Embassy of Guatemala; available: www.tuc.org.uk/research-analysis/reports/protest-re-killing-guatemala; accessed 5 August 2019). Chiquita pled guilty in 2007 to a criminal charge and was fined $25 m by the US authorities for its links to the right-wing paramilitary group the United Self Defense Forces of Colombia (AUC). Despite reaching agreements with trade unions in Latin America, allegations of human rights violations in Honduras, continue; see www.thenation.com/article/more-than-30-trade-unionists-have-been-killed-in-honduras-since-2009/ (accessed 5 August 2019).

58 Coca-Cola have been implicated in colluding with paramilitaries in "the systematic intimidation, kidnapping, detention and murder" of trade unionists in Colombia and Guatemala; see: www.theguardian.com/world/2001/jul/21/julianborger (accessed 5 August 2019).

59 BP's collusion with paramilitary death squads in Colombia is perhaps most notorious; see Lara Montesinos Coleman (2018) *Global Social Fascism: Violence, Law and 21st Century Plunder*, Centre for Global Political Economy Working Paper no. 15, Brighton: University of Sussex.

60 For example, in November 2017, Bangladeshi trade unions noted that at one of the country's largest manufacturers, Lakhsma Sweaters Ltd., "trade union leaders and activists are in constant fear of being a victim of forceful disappearance". Major buyers of Lakhsma Sweaters include BHS, Burton, Dorothy Perkins, Intersport and Primark. In 2018, a factory in India supplying the major brands H&M, Benetton, Abercrombie & Fitch and Columbia Sportswear was accused by the US NGO Worker Rights Consortium of threats of extreme violence against trade union organisers; see: www.theguardian.com/world/2018/jul/19/india-clothing-factories-shahi-exports-wrc-watchdog (accessed 5 August 2019).

61 For a summary, see Lara Montesinos Coleman, Gearóid Ó Loingsigh, Pierguisseppe Parisi, Gustavo Rojas-Páez and Owen Thomas (2019) *Righting Corporate Wrongs? Extractivism, Corporate Impunity and Strategic Use of Law*, London: War on Want.

62 P. Berryman, trans. (1993) *Report of the Chilean National Commission on Truth and Reconciliation*, Indiana: Notre Dame University; Peter Kornbluh (2004) *The Pinochet File: Atrocity and accountability*, New York: The New Press; Sampson, *The Sovereign State of ITT*.

63 M. Day (1975) Terror Increases in Chile as Opposition Movement Grows, *Los Angeles Free Press*, 7 March: p. 73.

64 Kwame Nkrumah (1965) *Neo-Colonialism: The Last Stage of Imperialism*, London: Panaf.

65 Nkrumah, *Colonialism*: pp. 52–53.

66 Nicholas Shaxson (2007) *Poisoned Wells: The Dirty Politics of African Oil*, New York: Palgrave Macmillan.

67 Nicholas Shaxson (2012) *Treasure Islands: Tax Havens and the Men Who Stole the World*, London: Vintage: pp. 157–158.

68 Michael Klare (2002) *Resource Wars: The New Landscape of Global Conflict*, New York: Henry Holt.

69 Greg Muttitt (2011) *Fuel on the Fire: Oil and Politics in Occupied Iraq*, London: The Bodley Head.

70 Greg Muttitt and David Whyte (2016) Chilcot's Blind Spot, *Open Democracy*, 6 July. Available: www.opendemocracy. net/en/opendemocracyuk/chilcot-s-oil-blind-spot-in-iraq-war-report/ (accessed 5 August 2019).

71 Peter Annin (2018) *The Great Lakes Water Wars*, Washington: Island.

72 Khoury and Whyte, *Corporate Human Rights Violations*.

73 Michael Parenti (2016) *The Face of Imperialism*, London: Routledge.

74 See also Vandana Shiva (2016) *Who Really Feeds the World? The Failures of Agribusiness and the Promise of Agroecology*, Berkeley: North Atlantic; Claude Ake (1981) *A Political Economy of Africa*, London: Longman.

75 Steven Shrybman (2000) *Trade, Agriculture, and Climate Change: How Agricultural Trade Policies Fuel Climate Change*, Minneapolis, Minnesota: Institute for Agriculture and Trade Policy.

76 Arundhati Roy (2001) *Power Politics*, Cambridge MA: South End Press: p. 20.

77 *The Hindu Business Line*, 31 August 2017. Available: www. thehindubusinessline.com/companies/cocacola-wants-to-make-india-its-thirdlargest-market-globally/article9838687. ece (accessed 5 August 2019).

78 War on Want (2006) *Coca-Cola: The Alternative Report*, London: War on Want.

79 Earth Talk (2019) Coca-Cola Charged With Groundwater Depletion and Pollution in India, Thought.co, 23 May. Available: www.thoughtco.com/coca-cola-groundwater-depletion-in-india-1204204 (accessed 5 August 2019).

80 *Guardian*, 18 June 2014.

81 I am grateful to Monish Bhatia for bringing the significance of this issue to my attention.

82 Meeta Ratawa Tiwary (2015) Impact of Disposed Drinking Water Sachets in Damaturu, Yobe State, Nigeria *International Journal of Environmental and Ecological Engineering*, vol. 9, no 10: pp. 1218–1221.

83 Dexter Galvin (2017) Deforestation: A Business-Critical Issue for the World's Biggest Buyers, CDP Online, 25 May. Available: www.cdp.net/en/articles/supply-chain/deforestation-a-business-critical-issue-for-the-worlds-biggest-buyers (accessed 5 August 2019).

84 Gabrielle Kissinger, Martin Herold and Veronique De Sy (2012) *Drivers of Deforestation and Forest Degradation: A Synthesis Report for REDD+ Policymakers*, Vancouver: Lexeme Consulting.

85 CDP (2016) *Revenue at Risk: Why Addressing Deforestation is Critical to Business Success*, London: CDP.

86 Verité (2013) *Risk Analysis of Indicators of Forced Labor and Human Trafficking in Illegal Gold Mining in Peru*, Amherst, Massachusetts: Verité.

87 David Hill (2018) Remote Amazon Tribe Hit by Mercury Crisis, Leaked Report Says, *Guardian*, 24 January.

88 Verité, *Risk Analysis of Indicators of Forced Labor and Human Trafficking*.

89 Perry Gottesfeld, Damian Andrew and Jeffrey Dalhoff (2015) Silica Exposures in Artisanal Small-Scale Gold Mining in Tanzania and Implications for Tuberculosis Prevention, *Journal of Occupational and Environmental Hygiene*, vol. 12, no. 9: pp. 647–653.

90 Gottesfeld et al., Silica Exposures in Artisanal Small-Scale Gold Mining in Tanzania.

91 Oscar Castilla, Nelly Luna Amancio and Fabiola Torres Lopez (2015) The Companies Accused of Buying Latin America's Illegal Gold, *Insight Crime* 4 August. Available: www.insight-crime.org/news/analysis/the-companies-accused-of-buying-latin-america-illegal-gold/ (accessed 5 August 2019).

92 Miriam Wells (2013) Breaking Down the Chain of Illegal Gold in Peru, *Insight Crime*, 11 December. Available: www.insightcrime.org/news/analysis/breaking-down-the-chain-of-illegal-peruvian-gold/ (accessed 5 August 2019).

93 Mark Curtis (2016) *The New Colonialism: Britain's*

Scramble for Africa's Energy and Mineral Resources, London: War on Want.

94 Curtis Research (2014) *Honest Accounts? The True Story of Africa's Billion Dollar Losses*. Available: www.francoph onie.org/IMG/pdf/honest-accounts_final-version.pdf (accessed 5 August 2019).

95 Alex de Waal, How to Steal From Africa, All Perfectly Legally, *African Arguments*, 6 May. Available: https://afric anarguments.org/2016/05/06/how-to-steal-from-africa-all-perfectly-legally/ (accessed 5 August 2019).

96 Curtis Research, *Honest Accounts?*

97 See also Damian Short (2016) *Settler Colonialism, Social Death and Ecocide*, London: Zed Books.

98 Klein, *This Changes Everything*: p. 176.

CHAPTER 3

1 BizLatinHub (2019) Use Free Trade Zones in Uruguay to Boost Your LATAM Business, 8 August. Available: www. bizlatinhub.com/free-trade-zones-in-uruguay-to-boost-yo ur-latam-business/ (accessed 15 August 2019). Free-trade zones are sometimes called "export processing" or "special economic" zones. In the context of Latin American, the companies operating in such zones are known as "maqui-las" or "maquiladoras".

2 *Merco Press* (2014) Uruguay Opens Second Pulp Mill with Annual Production Capacity of 1.45 Million Tons, 9 September. Available: https://en.mercopress.com/2014/09/ 09/uruguay-opens-second-pulp-mill-with-annual-product ion-capacity-of-1.45-million-tons (accessed 5 August 2019).

3 Steven Bittle (2012) *Still Dying for a Living*, Vancouver, BC: UBC Press; Raymond Michalowksi and Ronald Kramer (1987) The Space Between Laws: The Problem of Corporate Crime in a Transnational Context, *Social Problems*, vol. 34, no. 1: pp. 34–53; Rory O'Neill, Simon Pickvance and Andrew Watterson (2007), Burying the Evidence: How Great Britain is Prolonging the Occupational Cancer Epidemic, *International Journal of Occupational and Environmental Health*, vol. 4: pp. 428–436; Dawn Rothe

Notes

and David Friedrichs (2015) *Crimes of Globalization*, London: Routledge.

4 Michael Aglietta (2000) *A Theory of Capitalist Regulation: The US Experience*, London: Verso; see also Steven Bittle, and Lori Stinson (2019) Corporate Killing Law Reform: A Spatio-Temporal Fix to a Crisis of Capitalism?, *Capital and Class*, vol. 43, no. 2: pp. 251–270; and Fiona Haines (2011) *The Paradox of Regulation: What Regulation Can Achieve and What It Cannot*, Cheltenham: Edward Elgar.

5 Environment Agency (2018) *Regulating for People, the Environment and Growth*, Bristol: Environment Agency.

6 Ian Johnston (2017) UK company Sells Lead to Last Place on Earth Where Leaded Petrol is Legal, *Independent*, 22 August. Available: www.independent.co.uk/environment/leaded-pe trol-algeria-still-legal-innospec-cheshire-uk-sale-export-tel-tetraethyl-lead-a7907196.html (accessed 5 August 2019).

7 David Whyte (2004) All that Glitters Isn't Gold: Environmental Crimes and the Production of Local Criminological Knowledge, *Crime Prevention and Community Safety*, vol. 6, no. 1: pp. 53–63; actually this is not simply an issue for the island of Britain. The factory stands around 150 miles east of Dublin.

8 I have heard Steve make this point very powerfully, many times over, for many years. And it is a starting point for the analysis of the politics of regulation in our collaborative research.

9 Section 108.

10 Sara Reardon (2018) FARC and the Forest: Peace is Destroying Colombia's Jungle, *Nature: International Journal of Science*, 12 June. Available: www.nature.com/articles/d41586-018-05397-2 (accessed 5 August 2019).

11 Coleman, *Global Social Fascism*.

12 Jos Barlow and Alexander Lees (2019) Amazon Fires Explained: What Are They, Why Are They so Damaging, and How Can We Stop Them? *The Conversation*, 23 August.

13 Manuella Libardi (2019) Leaked Documents Show Brazil's Bolsonaro has Grave Plans for Amazon Rainforest, democraciaAbierta, 21 August.

14 *Financial Times*, 22 August, 2019.

Notes

15 Karl Marx [1887] (1954) *Capital: Volume 1*, London: Lawrence and Wishart: pp. 333–334.

16 Karl Marx, *Capital: Volume 1*: p. 229.

17 The double movement is a phrase coined by the economic sociologist Karl Polanyi in his book *The Great Transformation* to describe a dialectical process in which markets are opened up at the same time as they are regulated, for example, through the welfare state and other forms of social protection. The application of the term in this context suggests a similar process, but indicates a slightly different dialectic: a double movement that supports the development of different regulatory strategies with differing aims and political positions; Karl Polanyi (1962) *The Great Transformation: The Political and Economic Origins of Our Time*, Boston: Beacon.

18 E. Clark and K. Hermele (2013) *Financialisation of the Environment: A Literature Review* (FESSUD Papers; Vol. 17) Lund, Sweden: Lund University.

19 See, for example, report in the *Financial Times*, 23 September 2013. Available: www.ft.com/content/8f230656-21e0-11e3-bb64-00144feab7de (accessed 5 August 2019).

20 Environmental Justice Foundation (2003) *Smash & Grab: Conflict, Corruption and Human Rights Abuses in the Shrimp Farming Industry*, London: Environmental Justice Foundation.

21 Qiang Ji and Jian-FengGuo (2015) Oil Price Volatility and Oil-Related Events: An Internet Concern Study Perspective, *Applied Energy*, vol. 137, issue C: pp. 256–264; Christos Kolliasa, Catherine Kyrtsoub and Stephanos Papadamou (2013) The Effects of Terrorism and War on the Oil Price–Stock Index Relationship, *Energy Economics*, vol. 40, issue C: pp. 743–752.

22 David Whyte (2006) Regulating Safety, Regulating Profit: Cost Cutting, Injury and Death in the North Sea after Piper Alpha, in Eric Tucker (ed.) *Working Disasters: The Politics of Recognition and Response*, New York: Baywood.

23 Charles Woolfson, John Foster and Matthias Beck (1996) *Paying for the Piper: Capital and Labour in Britain's Offshore Oil Industry*, London: Mansell.

24 W.G. Carson (1981) *The Other Price of Britain's Oil*, Oxford: Martin Robertson.

25 Carson, *The Other Price of Britain's Oil*: p. 107.

26 Tombs and Whyte, *Safety Crimes*.

27 Pearce and Tombs, *Toxic Capitalism*.

28 Kristin Leutwyler (1998) The Last Sturgeon, *Scientific American*, 15 June. Available: www.scientificamerican.com/article/the-last-sturgeon/ (accessed 5 August 2019).

29 Maria Shahgedanova and Timothy P. Burt (1994) New Data on Air Pollution in the former Soviet Union, *Global Environmental Change*, vol. 4, no. 3: pp. 201–227; Klein, *This Changes Everything*.

30 See the World Health Organization resources on air pollution here: www.who.int/airpollution/en/ (accessed 5 August 2019).

31 A useful list of sources on those treaties is provided by the Georgetown Law Library. Available: https://guides.ll.georgetown.edu/c.php?g=273374&p=1824812 (accessed 5 August 2019).

32 Trade Union Congress (2010) *The Case for Health and Safety*, London: TUC.

33 For an overview of international inspection regimes, see Andrew Farmer (2007) *Handbook of Environmental Protection and Enforcement: Principles and Practice*, London: Earthscan.

34 This is according to analysis produced by the US campaign organisation, the Environmental Defence Fund. Available: www.edf.org/deep-epa-cuts-put-public-health-risk (accessed 5 August 2019).

35 Juliet Eilperin and Brady Dennis (2019) Under Trump, EPA Inspections Fall to a 10-Year Low, *Washington Post*, 8 February.

36 Dino Grandoni (2019) EPA's new "no surprises" inspection policy has some critics worried, *Washington Post*, 19 July.

37 *Reuters*, 19 July 2019.

38 Gary Lynch-Wood and David Williamson (2001) Regulatory Compliance: Organizational Capacities and Regulatory Strategies for Environmental Protection, in Hannah Quirk, Toby Seddon and Graham Smith (eds.) *Regulation and*

Criminal Justice: Innovations in Policy and Research, Cambridge: Cambridge University Press.

39 Environment Agency (2010) *Understanding and Improving SME Compliance*, Bristol: Environment Agency. For a critique of this position, see Whyte, An Intoxicated Politics of Regulation.

40 Gill Plimmer (2019) Can England's Water Companies Clean Up its Dirty Rivers? *Financial Times*, 12 June.

41 Steve Tombs (2016) *Social Protection After the Crisis: Regulation Without Enforcement*, Bristol: Policy Press.

42 Adam Vaughan (2018) BP's Deepwater Horizon Bill Tops $65bn, *Guardian*, 16 January.

43 BloombergNEF, 26 September 2019. Available: https://about.bnef.com/blog/liebreich-climate-lawsuits-existential-risk-fossil-fuel-firms/ (accessed 5 August 2019).

44 Ralph Atkins (2019) Beyer's $50 Billion Blunder, *Financial Times*, 8 August.

45 Phineas Baxandall and Ryan Pierannunzi (2013) *Subsidizing Bad Behavior: How Corporate Legal Settlements for Harming the Public Become Lucrative Tax Write Offs*, Washington: U.S. PIRG Education Fund.

46 Baxandall and Pierannunzi, *Subsidizing Bad Behavior*.

47 Grietje Baars (2016) It's Not Me, It's The Corporation: The Value of Corporate Accountability in the Global Political Economy, *London Review of International Law*, vol. 4, no. 1: pp. 127–163.

48 Jennifer Arlen (1994) The Potentially Perverse Effects of Corporate Criminal Liability, *The Journal of Legal Studies*, vol. 23, no. 2: pp. 833–867; Wallace Davidson III and Dan L. Worrell (1998) The Impact of Announcements of Corporate Illegalities on Shareholder Returns, *Academy of Management Journal*, vol. 31, no. 1: pp. 195–200; John Coffee Jr. (1980) Corporate Crime and Punishment: A Non-Chicago View of the Economics of Criminal Sanctions, *American Criminal Law Review*, vol. 17, no. 4: pp. 419–478.

49 Tombs and Whyte, *Safety Crimes*.

50 Sara L. Seck (2000) Environmental Harm in Developing Countries Caused by Subsidiaries of Canadian Mining Corporations: The Interface of Public and Private

International Law, *Canadian Yearbook of International Law*, vol. 37: pp. 139–221.

51 Anjli Raval and Leslie Hook (2019) Renewable Energy Push Barely Dents Fossil Fuel Dependence, *Financial Times*, 3 August.

52 Ron Bousso (2018) Big Oil spent 1% on Green Energy in 2018, *Reuters*, 12 November.

53 Ronald Coase (1960) The Problem of Social Cost, *Journal of Law and Economics*, vol. 3 (October 1960): pp. 1–44; Arthur Pigou (1932) *The Economics of Welfare*, 4th ed., London: Macmillan.

54 Klein, *This Changes Everything*.

55 Falk, Environmental Warfare and Ecocide, p. 20.

56 Joel Kovel (1997) The Enemy of Nature, *Monthly Review*, vol. 49, no. 6: pp. 6–14.

Conclusion

1 Malin Sahlin (2009) *Cutting the Edge – the Loss of Natural Forests in Sweden*, Stockholm: Swedish Society for Nature Conservation.

2 The tobacco firm Lorillard was bought by R.J. Reynolds in 2014. Asbestos firm Turner and Newall was bought by Federal-Mogul in 1998, which went bankrupt in 2001 largely as a result of asbestos claims.

3 Marie-Monique Robin (2012) *The World According to Monsanto*, New York: The New Press.

4 Diana Bronson, Hope Shand and Jim Thomas (eds.) (2011) *Earth Grab: Geopiracy, the New Biomassters and Capturing Climate Genes, Part 1*, Oxford: Pambazuka Press.

5 Karl Marx (1937) *The Eighteenth Brumaire of Louis Napoleon*, Moscow: Progress Publishers: p.10.

6 The term that geologists and earth scientists use for the epoch which signalled the commencement of significant human impact on Earth's geology and ecosystem.

7 InfluenceMap (2019) *Big Oil's Real Agenda on Climate Change*, London: InfluenceMap.

8 Frances Bowen (2014) *After Greenwashing: Symbolic*

Notes

Corporate Environmentalism and Society, Cambridge: Cambridge University Press.

9 *Financial Times*, 9 May 2019.

10 *BP commits $100 million to fund new emissions reductions project*, Press Release, 26 March 2019.

11 *Reuters*, 16 April 2018.

12 *Financial Times*, 3 December 2018.

13 Christophe McGlade and Paul Ekins (2015) The Geographical Distribution of Fossil Fuels Unused When Limiting Global Warming to 2°C, *Nature*, vol. 517: pp. 187–190.

14 In 2018, Shell's annual dividend was the largest in the world at $16 billion; ExxonMobil's, at $13.8 billion was the second largest; *Financial Times*, 8 November 2019.

15 Ben Chapman (2017) BP and Shell Planning for Catastrophic 5°C Global Warming Despite Publicly Backing Paris Climate Agreement, *Independent*, 27 October.

16 Mark Lynas (2008) *Six Degrees: Our Future on a Hotter Planet*, London: Harper Perenial.

17 *Financial Times*, 15 October 2019.

18 Bellamy Foster, Clark and York, *The Ecological Rift*; see also Frances Bowen, *After Greenwashing*.

19 Bloomberg News Online, Traders Say Rally In European Carbon Futures Won't End Soon, 10 October. Available: www.investors.com/research/options/carbon-futures-euro pe/ (accessed 5 August 2019).

20 McKenzie Funk (2014) *Windfall: The Booming Business of Global Warming*, New York: Penguin.

21 Funk, *Windfall*.

22 Naomi Klein (2007) *The Shock Doctrine: The Rise of Disaster Capitalism*, Toronto: Random House; and see updates in Naomi Klein (2019) *On Fire: The Case for a Green New Deal*, London: Allen Lane.

23 *Mirror*, 1 July 2019.

24 Martin Dorey (2018) *No. More. Plastic.*, London: Penguin: pp. 145–146.

25 Paul Griffin (2017) *The Carbon Majors Database: CDP Carbon Majors Report 2017*, London: CDP UK.

26 The breakdown is roughly as follows: 40% comes from selling air miles to credit card companies and other commercial

ventures; of the 60% passenger income, more than a third comes from business customers. From this perspective, even if non-business passengers were able to exert some collective demand to reduce the number of flights, they would have much less influence than commercial clients.

27 Clare Carlile (2019) History of Successful Boycotts. *Ethical Consumer*, 5 May. Available: www.ethicalconsumer.org/ethicalcampaigns/boycotts/history-successful-boycotts (accessed 5 August 2019).

28 This is my estimate based on figures reported by Australian academics Denise Hardesty and Chris Wilcox and reported by Seth Borenstein (2018) Science Says: Amount of straws, plastic pollution is huge, *AP*, 20 April.

29 Sandra Laville (2018) Greenpeace Says Retailers Failing to Take Responsibility for Reducing Footprint, *Guardian*, 15 November.

30 *Financial Times*, 16 August 2013.

31 Libby Peake (2018) *Less In, More Out*, London: Green Alliance.

32 Ann Pettifor (2019) *The Case for the Green New Deal*, London: Verso; Kate Aronoff, Alyssa Battistoni, Daniel Aldana Cohen and Thea Riofrancos (2019), *A Planet to Win: Why We Need a Green New Deal*, London: Verso.

33 For example, Common Wealth's detailed proposals argue that corporations "must be rewired through new forms of ownership and governance so that they are sustainable, democratic, and inclusive by design" without providing any detail about how this might be achieved. There are radical proposals for a national, publicly owned energy company, but in a number of Common Wealth's documents, more responsible corporations are at the heart of a Green New Deal. Labour for a Green New Deal, behind the UK Labour Party's proposals, seems to offer a more expanded model of public ownership, embracing energy, water and the railways. Yet, in those proposals, when it comes to challenging the entirety of corporate power, the focus is limited to those sectors; Johanna Bozuwa and Carla Skandier (2019) *Shifting Ownership for the Energy Transition in the Green New Deal: A Transatlantic Proposal*, London: Common Wealth;

Notes

Labour for a Green New Deal (2019) *Expanding Public, Democratic Ownership.* Available: https://static1.square space.com/static/5c742a3c77b9036ccae1eddf/t/5d721cbc 77a52f000186fedf/1567759550703/5+Expanding+public% 2C+democratic+ownership.pdf (accessed 5 August 2019).

34 The Greens/EFA Group in the European Parliament (2018) *Revolving Doors and the Fossil Fuel Industry: Time to Tackle Conflicts of Interest in Climate Policy-Making,* Brussels: The Greens/EFA Group in the European Parliament.

35 Corporate Responsibility (CORE) Coalition (2006) and the Trade Justice Movement Press Statement, 10 November.

36 BBC News, 1 February, 2017.

37 See also Baars, Capital, Corporate Citizenship and Legitimacy.

38 Mary Kreiner Ramirez and Steven A. Ramirez (2017) *The Case for the Corporate Death Penalty: Restoring Law and Order on Wall Street,* New York: NYU Press.

39 Michael Jefferson (2001) Corporate Criminal Liability: The Problem of Sanctions, *Journal of Criminal Law,* vol. 65: pp. 235–261.

40 Julia Kollewe (2018) RBS settles US Department of Justice Investigation With $4.9bn Fine, *Guardian,* 10 May.

41 Joel Bakan (2005) *The Corporation: The Pathological Pursuit of Profit and Power,* New York: Free Press.

42 David A. Ciepley (2013) Beyond Public and Private: Toward a Political Theory of the Corporation, *American Political Science Review,* vol. 107, no. 1, pp. 139–158.

43 Arundhati Roy (2014) *Capitalism: A Ghost Story,* Chicago: Haymarket: p 146.

44 UN Human Rights Council (2018) *Legally Binding Instrument to Regulate in International Human Rights Law, the Activities of Transnational Corporations and other Business Enterprises (zero Draft16.7.2018).* Available: www. ohchr.org/Documents/HRBodies/HRCouncil/WGTransCo rp/Session3/DraftLBI.pdf (accessed 5 August 2019).

45 David Nelken and Michael Levi (2018) Sir Philip Green and the Unacceptable Face of Capitalism, *King's Law Journal,* vol. 29, no. 1: pp. 36–57.

46 See the report by Pearl and Promise (2019) *As the Coal Industry Falls Apart, Miners Face Losing Their Pensions*, 2 August. Available: www.pbs.org/wnet/peril-and-promise/ 2019/08/coal-industry-falls-apart-miners-face-losing-their-pensions/ (accessed 5 August 2019).

47 For example, support for the principle of equity fines features in the following works: John Coffee (1981) "No Soul to Damn: No Body to Kick": An Unscandalized Inquiry into the Problem of Corporate Punishment, *Michigan Law Review*, vol. 79; John Braithwaite (1991) Penalties for White Collar Crime, AIC *Conference Proceedings*, 20–23 August, Canberra: Australian Government; Brent Fisse (1990) Sentencing Options Against Corporations, *Criminal Law Forum*, vol. 2; Harry J. Glasbeek (1984) Why Corporate Deviance is Not Treated as a Crime: The Need to Make "Profits" a Dirty Word, *Osgoode Hall Law Journal*, vol. 22: pp. 393–439; James Gobert and Maurice Punch (2003) *Rethinking Corporate Crime*, London: Butterworths; Neil Gunningham and Richard Johnstone (1999) *Regulating Workplace Safety: Systems and Sanctions*, Oxford: Oxford University Press.

48 Bellamy Foster, Clark and York, *The Ecological Rift*, p. 86.

49 Robert Knox (2010) Strategy and Tactics, *Finnish Yearbook of International Law*, vol. 21: pp. 195–229.

50 Ciepley, Beyond Public and Private.

Index

Index

Index

Index